No Victims
Only Survivors

No Victims Only Survivors

Ten Lessons for Survival

Deborah Scaling Kiley

For information about permission to reproduce selections from this book, write to Permissions, NVOS Publishing, 3904 West Vickery Boulevard, Fort Worth, Texas 76107.

Visit our website: www.novictimsonlysurvivors.com.

Library of Congress Cataloging-in-Publication data available.

ISBN 978-0-9778207-0-2

Printed in the United States of America.

For my husband Greg
and my children Marka, Quatro, Chelsea, and Alex
and
Parker, Rosie, Pearlene, and the fish
who have all taught me how to love and forgive.

Don't let your morale flag. Be daunted, but not defeated. Remember: the spirit, above all else, counts. If you have the will to live, you will. Good luck!

—Yann Martel, *Life of Pi*

A full life will be full of pain.

—M. Scott Peck, *The Road Less Traveled*

Contents

Acknowledgments

This was not a short-term project. It has taken me a lifetime to gather the information and put it on paper. And there have been so many people involved I'm sure I will forget someone. Forgive me if you are that person.

So here goes. I cannot imagine what my life would have been like without my children Quatro and Marka. They have been my greatest teachers and the most humbling forces in my life. I wish I could thank Grandmother Queenie for all her great wisdom and kindness, but I'm sure she has heard my prayers and knows how I feel. Many, many, thanks and great big hugs to Lu Jo Churchill and Bettie Galaway for standing in as mothers when mine was unable. Thanks to Daddy Jim for all the years he stuck in there. Thank you to my father Mike Galaway;

it has not always been easy for us, but I know you love me and I love you. And I love you, too, Bamama, even though you are the most hard-headed woman I have ever known.

Thanks to all my childhood friends and their parents, especially Mrs. Bourke; to Mame Gale and Della Daniel, my roommates in boarding school; and to Mr. Pittman. Thanks to my college buddies Lezlie Mitchell and Nancy Russell, both great examples of "No Victims, Only Survivors"; to my "around the world" buddy Rebecca Oswald; to Sarah and Brad Cavanagh. A very special thanks to Jan White and Judy Brodkin; I cherish your friendships more than you can imagine. Thanks to India Howell and our shared dream to change the world, and to Debbie Lewis, who always manages to bring us all together over the years. Julie French, I could not have made it without your wisdom and friendship.

A special thanks to Jana Posey, Yossi Ghinsberg, Dashelle Murrin, and Allison Montesi for lending their stories to this book. Kelli Cotten, your friendship reminds me daily that I am fearless. Thanks to Tom Wolf and Stephen Woodcock at Backwoods for all their help with the survival kit. Mary Jane Hooper—your wisdom and support have never failed me or our family—thank you for planting the seeds of change. A big hug to Theresa Brodigan. Laurence Gonzales, thank you for everything, especially for believing in the book from the beginning and for all your hard work and for introducing me to my new editor and soul sister Nita Congress. Thanks to the best, and most willing, proofreaders around: Genevieve Blackmon and Jean David. As for my pack of pound pets—Parker, Rosie, and Pearlene, who camp by my desk each day while I work—I treasure their love and loyalty.

To my mother: We cannot change the past and I'm not so sure I would even if I could. Know that I love you and wish that I could wash away the pain felt by two little girls from "the Bermuda Triangle of Texas" so many years ago.

Finally, I thank my husband Greg and all our children—Marka, Quatro, Chelsea, and Alex—for their love and support. Bottom line: I have the best family, friends, and life a woman could ask for.

preface

Gifts of Grace, Wrapped in Very Funky Paper

It was September 5, 2005, about eleven o'clock at night, and I was watching my husband Greg lug a new twenty-four-inch television set up three flights of stairs in an apartment building in Fort Worth, Texas.

Hurricane Katrina had just destroyed a big swath of the Gulf Coast, and we were taking in survivors. Greg and I had already donated money to the relief effort through the usual channels, but this was something else again, meeting real families with faces and feelings, joys and sorrows, and amazing tales of survival to tell. When you just write a check, you hope it does some good. But when you commit to taking in a real family, you don't hope: You know. Just that evening I had had a woman collapse in my arms, weeping with joy and gratitude.

Joy and gratitude? She had just lost everything she had.

The idea for the relief effort wasn't ours; it was Tish's, a young woman who had worked at the same gym where I teach yoga. A powerhouse of organization with her notebook with everybody's names and phone numbers, Tish, a single mother of four who's reclaiming and rebuilding her life after a childhood of abuse and indifference, is running this operation and she makes every dollar pay and pay. Tish is a survivor, nobody's victim, and she's doing what survivors do best: giving others the gift of survival.

She's the kind of person I like to be with these days.

A long and serious fight for survival led me to write this book. I had been shipwrecked at sea, and I don't mean metaphorically. I'd been a crew member on a boat that went down in a hurricane. I fought for my life for five days without food or water, fought sharks and despair and physical exhaustion. I watched three of my fellow crew members die, two of them eaten by sharks. And that was just the crowning incident in a lifetime of insanity. As a child, I'd escaped in the middle of the night from lunatics with guns. As a young woman, I'd come back from near death more than once, brought on by my bulimia. I'd overcome the wasting disease that a bad marriage can be too, and had put myself back through school and forged a life as a single mother. I had to go through all this before I was allowed to have the good life I now have.

Here's the biggest lesson I've taken from my survival: All those weird and terrible things that happened to me were gifts, gifts of grace—albeit gifts wrapped up in very funky paper. I would not give up one single moment of all that adversity for the cushy life I see some other people lead. Because without all I've gone through, my life wouldn't have the richness it has now.

And I don't just mean that in contrast to how terrible things were then that now is more precious. No. I literally mean that *because* then was terrible now can be wonderful. Like Tish, like every survivor I know, I have made *now* wonderful because I took the terrible of the past and ripped it apart, figured out what made it tick, looked for what it had to teach me, learned those lessons, made some new mistakes because I still didn't understand, and finally got it right.

No one wishes for adversity. But for every little mouse scurrying along on the ground, there is a hawk overhead, unseen. Bad things happen to everyone. And each time adversity dives in, it's an opportunity for growth. Every real survivor I've met has said just what I say: It was the best and worst thing that ever happened to them. My friend Jana, who was mauled and nearly killed by a giant saltwater crocodile, called her experience "a platform for growth." After years of surgery and therapy for her breast cancer, my friend Nancy told me, "I am blessed." And I can't tell you how many survivors coming out of Hurricane Katrina have told me how lucky they are. These people know a secret. I know it, too.

The secret to a rich life, a life lived completely, is knowing how to make the most of pain and turning adversity into growth.

It is a great paradox that the most destructive events in your life can be the most enriching and enlightening. In just one moment, you can descend into the abyss of being a victim—or rise to the victory of being a survivor.

We don't always get the choice, to be sure. There are planes that crash and earthquakes that shudder and fires that rage, and sometimes people are just in the wrong place at the wrong time. But too many people, when given the choice, the chance, to survive danger or succumb to it, choose victimhood. Not me. And not the people whose stories I tell in this book. And I hope not you.

At one time or another, we will all most probably be victims, put into a situation over which we have little or no control as it unfolds around us, enveloping us and threatening to overwhelm us. This could be disease, divorce, death, or destruction. But whatever it is, we need to see it as opportunity and use it, choose it, to make the transition from victim to survivor. And by making that choice, we receive the greatest gift—a lesson learned.

My forty-eight years of life have been a challenge since the day I was born. There have been many times that I thought I would never recover, that I'd always be a victim. But there was always that moment when I pulled myself out and kept on going.

I have a friend, India, who founded the Tanzanian Children's Fund. She says that she is trying to put herself out of business by educating the orphaned children in her village as well as the children in surrounding villages. She works to keep the children in their homes if they do have families, and, for those who are less fortunate, she provides a home and an education. This is India's way of teaching victims to be survivors and to in turn create a surviving, thriving country. I have countless other friends who work tirelessly for those whose lives have been touched by famine, diabetes, cancer, heart disease, child abuse, homelessness. They have a common goal: They work to turn victims into survivors.

Those of us who have been tested need to share our stories so that others can learn from our successes and our failures. As proof of this, I share with you this email I received last year:

> Deborah,
>
> I read your story yesterday. It was a good reminder of the extreme limits that the mind can take the body beyond. I am just past the halfway point of a year in Iraq flying helicopters for the Army. My adventure is not nearly so harrowing as yours but the mental process is similar. Positive attitude and breaking the task down into manageable pieces seem to be the key. It reads just like a chapter from any number of survival schools that I have attended with the military.
>
> Thanks for sharing your story. I too am finding out that the longer it stays inside the harder it becomes to share. I hope that you can take pleasure in knowing that... your story motivated me and helped me gain some perspective. Just five more months, one day at a time.
>
> Sincerely,
> Bryan Stokes
> Balad, Iraq

There's always a next struggle, always a new challenge; that's the nature of life. But believe me, it gets easier, especially if you learn the lessons as you go along. And the suffering—yes, there's always more suffering, too—becomes easier to take when you receive it as a gift and view it as an opportunity. In short, you can spend less time adrift at sea if you pay attention to the lessons and pay attention to what's going on in your own life and to how you make decisions.

Here are the ten lessons for survival I've learned from all my trials and tribulations:

1. *Awareness:* A keen sense of awareness is essential to survival. Know your surroundings. Believe what you see. Recognize the obstacles as well as the opportunities. In short: Pay attention.

2. *Intuition:* Intuition is real; it is the knowledge your soul holds for you. Believe in your *self*.

3. *Luck and Timing:* Luck and timing are gifts of grace wrapped in funky paper. Look for them and accept them. But remember, luck and timing favor the prepared mind.

4. *Preparation:* There is no substitute for being prepared. Being prepared mentally, physically, and spiritually are the keys to survival.

5. *Adaptability:* The world is in a constant state of change. Be willing to change old patterns and beliefs to fit your new and ever-changing world.

6. *Vision:* You must have a constant vision for your future. That vision can motivate you through the most difficult of times. A vision for the future creates the path for survival.

7. *Will:* The will to live means never, but never, giving up. There is always one more thing you can do to ensure the reality of your vision for the future.

8. *Accountability:* Life will hold you accountable for all your choices. To whom and for what do you want to be held accountable in life? Make every choice as if your life depended on it—because it does.

9. *Forgiveness:* All of us suffer. But it is how we react to the source of our suffering that determines whether we are vengeful or forgiving. Those who forgive are those who survive.

10. *Grace:* Grace is the pinnacle. It is a state of being where you see and feel the joy, the beauty, and, yes, even the humor, of the tests set before you. It is knowing that the lesson was worth learning and the life worth living.

This book is the story of how I learned these lessons, and how I came to my motto: "No victims, only survivors. Have passion for life."

one

The Bermuda Triangle of Texas

My childhood was not a pretty one, although the beginning does sound like a fairy tale.

My mother was the beautiful daughter of a wealthy rancher and oilman in the wild, low flatlands where the Red River divides Texas from Oklahoma. It was cattle country, an inhospitable land where money-hungry people went to take whatever they wanted and then take some more. When they'd taken what the land could give, they took the oil beneath it, and sometimes they even turned and took what belonged to others, too. And if you got in their way, they might even take your life. The towns there have names like Bowie and Gunsight and Medicine Mound, a reminder of the people who'd been killed off so someone else could get rich.

My husband and I call the area from just west of Abilene to Wichita Falls to just outside Fort Worth "The Bermuda Triangle of Texas," because it sometimes seems that everybody there is just a little bit crazy, and some of them quite a bit more. Not surprisingly, I was born smack dab in the middle of it—Olney, Texas.

When my mother was a teenager growing up in that area, she was sent away to Hockaday, a very fancy girls' boarding school in Dallas. She didn't stay long; for some reason, she quickly returned to west Texas and her wealthy father—and her mother too, of course.

During high school in Abilene, she caught the eye of a sweet and gentle boy—a college student named Mike Galaway—who also happened to be a sometime bull rider and a ranch hand. She got pregnant by him, and, dutiful Christian that my father was, he married my seventeen-year-old mother and went to work on her father's ranch.

I was born on January 21, 1958, and the very next year, my mother told Mike that she didn't need him anymore, because her father was going to take care of her. In fact, her father was taking care of her in a way that only a few people knew about at the time—which may explain why she came back from boarding school so soon. When my father would come home from work, he'd find my grandfather "Pawpoo" and Mother in the house acting sheepish, like they were hiding something. After she divorced my father, she rarely allowed me to see him again, possibly to keep him from telling me what he saw. Years later, he would confirm what my mother's mother had told me: Way out on that isolated ranch, with all his money, Pawpoo could have had any number of women. He chose his daughter instead.

⁂

After disposing of my father, my mother married again to a man I called Daddy Jim. She soon had another child, Lee, and, a few years later, divorced Daddy Jim, too. Mother, Lee, and I moved to Fort Worth, and there she met another rich oilman, this one from a small town just outside of Wichita Falls, Texas. She soon married him, too. I had barely started school when he whisked us away from Fort Worth and moved us to his isolated ranch in the Bermuda Triangle area. And then things really started getting crazy.

The drinking would start early and go late. The yelling would begin, and the guns would come out. Somehow I'd find myself in the middle of it, and then the belts would come off and they'd beat me until I had bleeding welts and bruises. But children are very resourceful, and I quickly learned how to read the signs. It was as if there was something inside me guiding me, protecting me. Based on the subtle signals of voice or gesture, *It*—that thing inside me—would tell that this was going to be a stormy night, and I'd simply disappear. Disappearing became my special gift, and *It* was my guide.

I'd hide out in the barn with the horses, and, if it was too cold out there, I'd hide in the attic. My mother had an old cedar chest, and I was told never to go near it, so of course I did. I'd turn out the light and crawl inside and shut the lid. I had a special way of sticking an old white leather glove just where the lock was so that I wouldn't get locked in and so that I could hear if anyone was coming. Because I knew there was no help, no one to turn to but myself. We were all alone out there on the Texas plains, and everyone was crazy but me. So I'd lie there smelling the sharp, sweet aroma of cedar, and I'd pray to God to make me happy when I grew up. Every night of my life as a child, I prayed for that. I could see that other people had great lives. It didn't seem right. "Dear God," I'd say, "I don't care how bad it gets while I'm little. I know I can take it now. But please, can I please be happy when I grow up?"

The one respite from that insanity came on weekends, when my brother Lee's father, Daddy Jim, would take me with them either to his house in Wichita Falls or to visit Lee's grandmother in Montague. She was known as Grandmother Queenie, and she took a special liking to me. She provided the vital human contact my own mother couldn't, or wouldn't, provide. Grandmother Queenie would take me to the creek to catch crawfish behind her house in Montague, where her husband, Granddaddy Buck, was the sheriff. We had a secret place we'd go to along the creek bed. It was protected by a huge arch of trees and vines that had grown up overhead. During the blistering hot summers, it was cool and dark in there, the sunlight barely leaking through. I felt safe in there with the wildlife and the berries that we'd pick and eat.

Grandmother Queenie was a kind woman, a great cook, and very religious. But most important, she paid attention to me. She cared about me. She fed me and mended "rubby" blanket (that's what I called the little blanket I carried around as a small child). I hated to take naps, and she forced me to do it, but even that was a sign that it mattered to her what I did and what happened to me. And more than food or money or clothes or even education, that's what children need: Someone who truly cares what happens to them.

The trips to Grandmother Queenie's would always end on Sunday night. And then Lee and I would go back to the ranch, where things were not at all what they appeared to be to the outside world. And as we approached the dusty road that led to that remote house, I could feel the dread settle in my gut, knowing what was going to happen. *Its* vacation was over.

My new father was rich, powerful, and crazy. He was a heavy drinker who would lock himself in my bedroom with a gun and masturbate. I'd go to bed and be trying to sleep when he'd come in, reeking of alcohol and sweat, carrying a loaded .357 Magnum. He'd drape his hand over my shoulder and lie in bed next to me, playing with himself. And something inside of me—the self that was me—would just disappear, go floating away over the sea of pretty cabbage roses on the dark carpeting of my room. If I couldn't literally disappear into the barn or the cedar chest, then I could magically disappear into my mind and leave my body behind. When my mother would start yelling and beating on the door with her fists, I'd barely hear her. "What are you doing in there!" she'd shriek, "Oh my God!" She knew, of course. She'd been through it herself when she was a girl. And no matter how far she tried to run from her father, she always seemed to run right back into the suffocating grip of the very same sort of man. Only now he wasn't interested in her. He was interested in me. And he liked me so much that he even legally adopted me.

A child in the third grade doesn't understand concepts like adoption, child support, divorce. So it was very confusing to me when my mother told me that I couldn't see my real father anymore because he had given me up for adoption to the man in my bedroom with the loaded gun. Then she asked me how I felt about that. I could only imagine that my real father mustn't really love me if he gave me up. I was miserable. All I really wanted was to have my father back, my real father. But this new one—the one who came to my room to masturbate—he must like me more, or else he wouldn't have adopted me. I could feel my small world closing in on me, becoming dangerously crazy. I just held on at night, telling myself I could take it, and prayed.

Mother of course, divorced again, and this time she explained that it was because of me that she'd had to do it. This was typical of the crazy things she'd say. She didn't divorce him because of me. She divorced him because he was even crazier than she was. In the final incident, he left our house late at night, insanely drunk, and drove off to his father's ranch to try to kill him with a shotgun. As he left our ranch, he backed out right over my two new puppies and killed them both. He drove to his father's ranch down the road, shot out all the tires of his dad's pickup truck, and then tried to run him over with his own truck.

We found this out because the Texas Highway Patrol came out to the house to warn my mother that he was on his way back to kill her, too. The police couldn't protect her from him, because she wasn't willing to press charges against her husband. So they just told her to get out, and that's what we did.

When you're a rich Texan, that's the way things work. And the casual way people use guns is another artifact of that way of life: He had a scar from where it was rumored his own mother had once shot him. So in the middle of the night, without even packing, my mother, Lee, and I left the house, got in the car, and drove straight to Vail, Colorado. That was the very last time I ever saw my mother's third husband, my new legal father.

That became our pattern: Every time my mother changed husbands, the geography changed, too, from the ranch to Wichita Falls to Fort Worth to Vail and then back to Fort Worth again. She was single for a while at that time and a real wild one. Her best friend was Priscilla Davis, who was married to Cullen Davis, one of the richest men in Texas. Cullen Davis was the model for J.R. Ewing in the television series *Dallas*.

Much later, one night in the summer of 1976, Priscilla's daughter Andrea (from a previous husband) was alone in Priscilla's six-million-dollar house in Fort Worth, while her mother was out with a college basketball star, Stan Farr. They were celebrating Priscilla's divorce from Cullen. I knew Andrea and her older sister, Dee, well. I used to be Andrea's baby-sitter and had spent many nights in that twenty-room mansion with the two girls. Andrea was a gentle, intelligent girl, who had somehow transcended the viciousness of the people around her. She looked like a baby Audrey Hepburn, a fairy-tale child who just stole your heart with her sweetness.

If I hadn't been away at boarding school, I might well have been in the house with her that night, when a man dressed in black and wearing a wig entered the house, took her to the basement, forced her to kneel on the floor, and shot her in the back of the head. When Priscilla walked in, the gunman shot her in the chest. Before he could finish the job, Farr came in and was shot four times and killed, while Priscilla managed to run out of the house. When a young couple stumbled onto the scene (in time to hear Priscilla call her attacker "Cullen"), the gunman shot the boy, crippling him for life. Priscilla survived, and Cullen Davis was tried for murder—but not convicted.

That was the world I grew up in, and none of this strange stuff seemed so out of the ordinary. It seemed wrong, certainly. It was terrifying, to be sure. But things like that were happening all the time, and they're still happening today. Only about two years ago, the husband of a distant cousin killed his three children and then shot himself. The children were two, four, and six, and I had to take my grandmother to the funeral and see those three tiny coffins.

When my mother divorced her third husband, amid gunfire and dead dogs and hurried escapes in the middle of the night, I was in fourth grade. By the time we felt safe enough to move back from Vail to Fort Worth, it was 1971, and I was now in the fifth grade. The drinking had always been there; I had never really known life without it. From my great-grandfather to Pawpoo to Mother and who knows who else in between, they were all big drinkers. But it was when all the prescription pill bottles starting showing up (or maybe I just started noticing them) that things got even crazier.

It became difficult to have friends, because their parents were frightened, disturbed, or disgusted by my mother's behavior. When a friend told me she couldn't come and spend the night with me because of my mom, I was humiliated. I remember the words "lewd and lascivious behavior" being used at some point and time—I think by someone whose father was a lawyer. And when I fell in love with a boy in the seventh grade, his parents kept us apart because of my mother.

Out of the blue, I was offered a reprieve from the worst of the insanity. My brother Lee's father, Daddy Jim, was living in Fort Worth, too, and I was allowed to accompany Lee to his house on weekends. Daddy Jim treated me just like his own daughter. He bought my school clothes and paid for my ballet lessons. He even bought me a horse. Daddy Jim soon remarried. His new wife was Lu Jo, and she had two young daughters. Lu Jo took me under her wing and taught me how to needlepoint and cook. For the first time since Grandmother Queenie, I had a mother figure who was really there for me, giving me unconditional love during some really difficult times. Naturally, my mother hated her. But Lu Jo protected me the best she could from the craziness of Mother's lifestyle.

Within a few years, Daddy Jim took custody of Lee, and I was faced with one of the greatest decisions of my life. When I was about thirteen or fourteen, Daddy Jim asked me if I wanted to come live with him and Lee and Lu Jo. And my heart said yes—a thousand times yes. It was what I wanted more than anything else in the world, what I'd prayed for—a real, loving family.

But there was a problem. A big problem.

Despite her constant badgering of me—I was too fat, my hair was too stringy, I talked too much, I was too loud, I was too quiet—and despite how scary she could be when she was drunk or high—I couldn't leave my mother. I was afraid she'd commit suicide or something after losing Lee. I felt I had to stay and take care of her.

Many years later, after refusing to leave the crew of what was obviously a doomed ship—and after being cast away at sea as a result—I developed a saying for myself: I don't do sinking ships. Refusing to leave my mother at that crucial moment in my life was virtually the same as staying on a sinking ship. This is how we learn to make good decisions: By making really bad ones.

It was around that time, during my transition from childhood into womanhood, that my mother was dating a guy who owned racehorses. I had always loved horses. When I had to hide in the barn, I was comforted by their beauty and grace and power. Now I was thrilled because we got to have lunch with some of the jockeys. And I overheard them talking about the fact that if they happened to be a little overweight before a race, they could simply make themselves throw up and dump the excess weight.

This struck me as an ingenious solution to one problem I had with my mother. She was always telling me I was overweight, along with telling me that my hair was wrong, that I wasn't pretty enough, smart enough, cute enough, good enough. Well, I reasoned, throwing up could at least make me thin. I was going to fix my relationship with my mother by making myself perfect, starting from the outside. I thought I'd hit on the perfect strategy.

I was about fourteen years old when I first started making myself throw up. There was something deeply satisfying in that kind of control. I had a new power, and it was all mine. No one in the world could touch it or take it away from me. I could eat anything I wanted, and it would simply go away. It was also an intense physical experience, and I was already well along in my search for intense physical experiences to fill the empty space in me. (I had first dropped acid in sixth grade.) In addition, the feeling it gave me quieted the endless anxiety I felt. It made me feel that I could control my relationship with my mother, fix it by making myself worthy. By the time I realized that it wasn't working, I was fully addicted to the bingeing and purging of bulimia. And I'd never even heard the word.

It was somewhere around a year or so later that my birth father, Mike, contacted me. He had remarried a woman with three boys and was living on a small ranch outside of Abilene. He wanted to see me. Life was just getting more confusing.

My mother was forever trying to get rid of me so that she could live her life unfettered and uninterrupted. The truth is, if I had spent my life with my mother, I'd probably be completely crazy by now. Fortunately, she wasn't very interested in me, so I spent a lot of time with other people.

As the years went on and her drinking and drug-taking got worse, it became more and more obvious that I wasn't wanted around. When I was in grade school, I'd be sent off to camp during the summers. When my mother wanted to get away, she'd just travel and leave me with whomever would have me. For a time, my mother's mother, whom I called Bamama, would come and stay with me when my mother traveled. But as my mother's behavior grew more erratic, even Bamama refused to come. She didn't approve of my mother sleeping with married men.

For my part, I was becoming proficient in the family lifestyle of drinking and drugs. By the time I was in tenth grade, my mother could no longer figure out what to do with me. And as always, I was cramping her style. So she sent me away to boarding school in Colorado Springs.

At first, getting away from her and the crazy people she knew seemed like one of the best things that had ever happened to me. For the first time in my life, I was spending every day, all day, with normal people. Or at least they seemed normal compared to the ones I'd grown up with. There were plenty of bulimic girls at school, so I fit right in. And I told all the girls how wonderful my mother was. Some of them told me how great their mothers were, too.

But here's the really bizarre part: I started to miss her. Intensely. The more I told those girls about home, the more I wanted to go back to the home I was describing. A fantasy home really. Because even though I knew I wouldn't really enjoy it if I did go back, I wanted to be home with her. The very thing that was worst for me was what I craved most, and I was desperately attracted to the very person who could hurt me the deepest. I was willing to do anything to get back home from boarding school. I must have been crazy.

The first thing I tried was stealing. I thought if I got caught stealing, I'd be expelled and sent home. I stole a piece of jewelry and hid it in the dresser in my dorm room. By the time I was caught, I'd changed my mind, though, and denied stealing it. No one really believed me. But they didn't send me home either.

Drugs were plentiful at the boarding school, and one day, on speed, I decided that I couldn't stand it any longer, so I ran away, thinking that now they would send me home for sure. They didn't. They sent me to a psychiatrist, who listened patiently to my story. I thought I was giving him a pretty tame account of my life—the drinking and drugs, the abuse, the guns, the constant running due to the multiple marriages—and was a bit puzzled when he told me what was wrong with me: He said that I'd seen and been through more than most fifty-year-olds. No wonder I was screwed up.

In 1974, the year my mother sent me away to boarding school, she married yet again. When I went home for spring vacation, her new husband gave me a brand-new white Pontiac LeMans with a vinyl top for my belated seventeenth birthday. I immediately took it out into the mountain roads on the way to Vail—and totaled it.

It wasn't a cry for help or anything like that. I was listening to Crosby, Stills, Nash, and Young and not paying any attention when I hit a patch of black ice, spun the car twice, and went carroming off the guard rail.

Looking back on it now, I see how close I came to death. I also see that this was just the latest example of running without a destination to head to.

❧

Within a year of her fourth marriage, my mother divorced again. She moved to Colorado Springs, where I was in boarding school. She'd show up at my dorm, drunk out of her mind, and take me and my friends out to dinner.

At least I had her back. Sort of.

❧

I graduated from high school in 1976 and moved to Reno with my mother and her latest husband—number five—a rancher from Nevada. Like my mother when she'd been my age, I fell in love with a bull rider and spent a pleasant summer following him to rodeos up and down the West Coast. I gave him my virginity, but when I went to Texas Tech that fall in Lubbock, we broke up.

A lot of my friends from Fort Worth were there. Throwing myself back into that old group after having been away in boarding school for two years was more than I could handle. There was just too much old baggage, too many reminders, and my bulimia accelerated to a new level of intensity, with my weight dropping to a dangerous eighty-two pounds. Weakened, I caught the chicken pox. While that disease is not usually serious for little children, it can be deadly for an adult or young adult, especially one with a compromised immune system.

I called my mother and explained that I had to come home, that I was sick, but she refused to take me back. She said her marriage wasn't going well (big surprise there). I'm sure she had no idea how intense the pain of her rejection was, had always been. Her own emotional machinery had been too badly damaged when she was a child, and now she was too deep in her own world of drinking and drugs to feel anything at all for me.

That's when I turned to my father—my real father, my mother's original bull rider. Without telling my mother, I had been in touch with him and his new wife Bettie for a number of years. Before I was sent away to boarding school, I received a call at home late one January night. A boy's voice on the line said, "Your father is my stepfather, and he'd really love to see you." We knew my mother would never allow it, so we agreed to meet in secret, and we continued doing so for years.

Many times while I was in boarding school, my mother wouldn't let me come home during vacations. If she was busy or didn't want to be bothered, she'd tell me to find someplace else to go, assuming I'd stay with friends from school. Instead, I'd go stay with Bettie and my father; and, for the second time in my life, I not only had someone who acted like a mother, but I got a real taste of what life is—or can be—for a normal family.

My father worked as a cowboy, and they lived on a tiny ranch near Abilene. Even though I was from a rich family, I wasn't a rich girl—though a lot of people didn't realize that. My mother's family didn't give me money, although they did give me a lot of the stuff that money can buy: fancy clothes, cars, food. I'm not sure why they were so tight with their money, but it's probably just as well. Because in my experience, money tends to do for unhappiness what it does for bad taste: It makes it worse—and my family had both.

So I may have had everything money could buy, but my father's family had all the things that couldn't be bought. Like love and common sense. They didn't drink much for one thing. And they didn't take everything for granted. Life was not handed to them on a silver platter, and so they valued it differently. We'd go fishing in order to catch fish, because we needed to eat. I'd have to go out to the barn to catch a chicken if we were going to have it for dinner. There was a practical, yet deeply spiritual, side to their lives that I'd rarely seen.

Then, during one of these vacations, my mother called the school looking for me, and they told her that I'd gone to my father's home. And she went nuts, screaming at me on the phone, "How could I have anything to do with that man who gave you up for adoption to a child abuser?" For a brief moment I thought she cared. But it was just manipulation, all about control. I found out later that shortly after they'd divorced, she'd sent my father a letter telling him he needn't pay any child support. Then a few years after that, she sent him another letter saying that he could either pay the back child support he owed—more than ten thousand dollars—or her new husband (the one who turned out to be the child abuser) would adopt me. Again, it was all about manipulation and control.

By the spring of 1977, when I was in quarantine with chicken pox, my father had moved his family from the ranch near Abilene to San Angelo, Texas, and so that's where I went when my mother rejected me.

Yet even then I wasn't willing to give up on her. I was too stubborn for that.

I fought my way back to health and eventually got my weight back up to ninety-seven pounds. I went to San Angelo State

University because it was close and I needed to get my grades good enough to enroll at the University of Texas in Austin. All this time, it seemed as if the life I was fighting for, the light at the end of the tunnel, was so close, yet just out of reach. I knew I was smart. I never had trouble making good grades. I'd graduated as vice president of my high school class. And I'd been doing well at Texas Tech in Lubbock. I made the dean's list at San Angelo. But each time, some invisible force seemed to yank me back and destroy all my progress. I began to wonder if it was some outside force or just self-destruction. At Texas Tech, it was my bulimia, making me too sick to go on. In Austin, it was something else again.

While at Austin, I was studying anthropology by day and working as a waitress in a honky-tonk joint at night. Mother wasn't paying for college, and my father didn't have the money, so I was on my own and had to work. It was a pretty good job, but members of a local motorcycle gang had begun to hang out there. They were, I was quick to discover, a group of guys who had more tattoos than teeth, and they were under investigation for a number of area murders. I got the crazy idea that I should do a paper on them for school. It would make a unique anthropological or sociological study, I thought, never considering the dangers involved.

Growing up with people who shot each other, drank all the time, and abused their children, I didn't always make good decisions; I had never really learned how to read the cues around me about what was and wasn't good for me. As further proof of this, I didn't tell anyone about the paper I planned to write for school. It was like some unconscious part of me knew it was an insane idea, because if I had told someone, they would have said, "Are you nuts? Those guys could kill you."

And they nearly did.

I started hanging out with them, and they accepted me. I also started keeping a journal so that I could write my paper. Then one day, my roommate read my journal and ratted me out to the gang. When I showed up at their place that night, they beat me to within an inch of my life and put me in the hospital for a couple of days. Why my roommate told them, I'm not sure, but I do know this: Growing up with crazy people makes it difficult to learn how to choose healthy companions later.

It was January 1979, and recognizing the danger I was in I called my uncle Ross (my mother's brother: Mother was nowhere to be found) and told him the situation. He had me sign some papers in regard to the ranch and set up an account at the local bank in west Texas, and so now I had a little money. I immediately dropped out of school in my junior year and flew, on impulse, to St. Thomas in the Caribbean. I'd obviously internalized my mother's fight-and-flight pattern from her many escapes after bad marital decisions. And, in line with my own poor decision-making skills, I told no one where I was going.

I checked into a hotel and got a job as a cook on a charter boat, a nice sixty-foot yacht crewed by a gorgeous guy named Cochise. We immediately hit it off. Looking back, I think that was probably because he was screwed up in the exact same way I was. He'd been a helicopter gunner in Vietnam and had terrible nightmares. He'd wake up screaming. There was a very dark place inside of him that matched a very dark place inside of me, and we recognized each other as kindred spirits. There was also a very tender place in him that matched the deep and loving nature I had inside me. We started a sweet, gentle romance, and, when he sailed off to Antigua for Race Week, I sailed with him. It was great for a while. Everyone liked Cochise, and I was Cochise's girl.

After I'd been gone about four months, it occurred to me that no one knew where I'd disappeared to. When I finally did call my mother, though, she acted as if nothing out of the ordinary had happened. She hadn't even missed me. I figured that she wouldn't even notice if I died. I thought about calling my dad, but he and Bettie had had another child while I was in college. We were at completely different stages of life—not to mention the fact that we came from two completely different worlds.

So: no mother, no father. This realization propelled me with an even greater force on my run into oblivion. If no one was going to miss me, I reasoned, it made no difference where I went. Anything was possible. And since every effort I'd made toward any normal kind of success was sabotaged by that dark invisible force within me, I might as well continue to follow my nose and see where it led. Why not just let *It* be my guide? What was the worst thing that could happen? I supposed I could die, but *It* had protected me this far. I plunged ahead.

In Antigua I said goodbye to Cochise, and signed on to deliver a yacht across the Atlantic Ocean. Another terrific decision, exactly the one that got a girl I'd come to know a few years later killed: Take to the open ocean with people you hardly know. Maybe that's what I secretly wanted.

My state of mind was such that I don't even remember where I boarded the boat, a clumsy forty-foot ketch made out of concrete, called *The Rolling Stone*. I joined the crew with the promise of either a job at the other end or a plane ticket home, but neither materialized when I arrived. So I found myself, at age twenty-two, alone and broke on the streets of London.

It was a weekend when I arrived, and no banks would open until Monday, so I couldn't even wire home for money. All the youth hostels were filled. With nowhere to go, I went to the police. By chance, the London coroner happened to be there and caught wind of my situation. He had several daughters, and his wife later told me that he decided to take me in because he hoped that someone would have done the same for his girls if they ever found themselves in my situation (God forbid). They were a wonderful family, and the next day they even helped me get some money wired to England. I boarded a train bound for Portsmouth, where I'd left my things after my first Atlantic crossing.

The fact that it was a coroner who took me in didn't strike me as grimly fitting until much later. I had effectively ended my life, obliterated myself, and I'd wound up with the coroner of London. I was floating from place to place like a ghost.

It took me years to appreciate that seemingly chance encounters and events are more than just that. I use the words "synchronicity" and "serendipity" to describe the phenomenon, but I also call it God. There's a universal force directing events. And if you're paying attention, you can see it happen almost every day of your life.

For example, on the train to Portsmouth, I met a man. He was from the U.S., and he was the project manager for the American entry in the Whitbread Around the World Race. For someone who was running to nowhere, this man seemed to provide me with the perfect opportunity. I told him I'd like to sail in that race.

Of course, the idea was outrageous. What I knew about sailing I'd only learned since coming to the Caribbean a few months ago, albeit with a few bouts on some snake-infested lakes in Texas in my childhood. I was hardly experienced. I had no credentials, either. Also, I was a woman, and few women had ever sailed in the Whitbread before. The American told me it would never happen—as any person with a set of normal emotional cues would have figured out immediately.

There are both advantages and disadvantages to being as out of touch with reality as I was. In this case, his refusal only solidified my crazy resolve to prove him wrong and get in the race. The fact is, I loved the ocean, and when the sailing was good, as it had been with Cochise, I had really found peace there.

On the train, I was able to pick the American's brain and learn that the South African team was having trouble finding crew members and that the boats were all in dry dock in Swanage, which was not too far from Portsmouth. After a stop in Portsmouth to pick up my stuff, I headed for Swanage and found the South African boat, *Xargo III*, being prepared for the race.

Having learned from some of the best pathological liars in Texas, I was able to overcome all the objections the South Africans threw at me and talk my way into a spot as a cook on their boat. I wasn't a trained cook either, but I had cooked with my grandmother since I was a little girl, and no one on the charter boat had complained, so I figured I could handle it.

The race was carried out in four legs and lasted a year, and I was the first American woman ever to finish it. I probably set another sort of record by being the first woman to finish it while suffering from bulimia. On a sixty-five-foot boat with eleven other people, your share of space is about six square feet, sometimes less, so this was quite a trick to pull off, especially when food and water were rationed. But I did it.

I also managed occasional radio contact with my mother, who was now living in New Orleans, renewing my vain hope of establishing some sort of relationship with her.

When the race was over, I found myself in Paris, where I was asked to sail in a race from La Rochelle, France, to New Orleans. It was an all-female crew, and they were all French except me and one other American, Sarah Cavanagh.

The French women on that crew were mainly dinghy sailors, while Sarah and I were used to big boats and open seas. As a result, though the weather was good, all the French women were incapacitated by seasickness halfway into the race, leaving Sarah and me to sail the boat alone. Decades later, Sarah and I both count that experience as one of the most satisfying moments in our lives. Of course, though, as soon as the French women got over being seasick, they took back control of the boat from us "beginners."

We arrived in New Orleans thirty-seven days later, coming in second in the all-female division. By then, I had started getting cold feet about seeing my mother. Of course, I longed for her more than anything else in the world—that is, I longed for a person she could never be. And by now, I knew how painful the experience was going to be. But our crew was attracting a lot of media attention, and Sarah convinced me that I had to call my mother or she'd find out from the television coverage that I was in town.

It was actually a great reunion, at first. That's the pattern with my mother. She took us out to dinner and came to all the post-race parties with me and Sarah. And I followed my pattern, too, raising my hopes higher and higher that I might finally discover the mother I'd always longed for. When the parties ended, when Sarah went home to Massachusetts and the race crowd dispersed and the media went away, my mother informed me that I'd worn out my welcome and asked when I'd be leaving.

Her rejection was a crippling blow—all the more so because I hadn't expected it. Each time, I was sucked back in, set up by the same emotions. Until I was able to see all this clearly, to lead an examined life, I was doomed to repeat those patterns. I had many trials before me.

Exhausted from bulimia and from two years of almost continuous sailing, from constant running, and from a long history of sabotaged lunges at success, I packed a few things and left New Orleans on a northbound bus with absolutely no idea of where I was going. I wasn't even kidding myself any longer that I had a plan of some sort. Sarah had accidentally left her passport behind, and I had the vague idea that I'd bring it to her, though, of course, I could easily have just mailed it. I was just moving to move, to put miles between me and my mother, between me and my heartache. But I was really just running from something that was all the time inside me.

I reached Rowley, Massachusetts, a week later and stayed with Sarah for a few days. I met her brother Brad, who was also a sailor, while I was there. I then continued north with no real plan other than the vague recognition that I'd have to decide on something soon, because I'd reached the end of the United States.

In Portland, Maine, I bought an Army surplus pup tent and continued up the coast to Bar Harbor and a tourist area on Mount Desert Island. I arrived with $3.58 in my pocket, knowing no one, having no prospects. Somehow it didn't even register that I was homeless. Of course, if I'd thought about it more deeply at the time, I'd have realized I'd been homeless all along, since I was born to a homeless mother who could offer no safe retreat because she herself had never known one.

Wandering the earth like in an old fairy tale, with no ties to a home or family, I was on my way to meet my fate, the most horrible and valuable experience of my life, which would transform all that had gone before and illuminate it with meaning and make me whole. It was a journey I could not have planned, no matter how clever I was, because it wasn't one that could be imagined. All my previous efforts at success, at somehow winning my mother over, transforming her, transforming me through bulimia or school or work or some other addictive behavior—they were all sideline distractions. Of course, I couldn't know any of that at the time.

It was June 1982 when I arrived in Bar Harbor, and I once again talked my way into a job right at the bottom of the food chain: Cleaning rooms in a small motel. The owner promised me the job if I'd get a real place to live instead of a tent. I had seen a sign for a room to rent over a convenience store and went straight there, again using my powers of persuasion: I told the man about the job I'd just gotten and promised to pay him in a week. He agreed, and I was once again set up in a temporary place in the world.

I've always been good at this part, these so-called ordinary things that people do, like working and making money or going to school and making good grades. But the secret force inside me always found some way to trip me up, to take me past the safe and secure route and out to the edge.

I worked and saved and moved up to a better job, a better place to live. I wound up as a waitress at the best place in town, Bubba's. As fall approached, I had managed to put twenty-three hundred dollars in the bank. It was just after Labor Day, early September 1982, and this seasonal town was about to close for the winter. I was being pushed toward a decision of some sort. Winters up there could be hard, with less work and more bills to pay. I decided I needed to move south. Once again, I thought, if I could just get to New Orleans...

And that's when I heard about a ship's captain named John Lippoth, who was taking a boat named *Trashman* from Southwest Harbor, Maine, to Florida on a routine yacht delivery. It would be a free ride south, and, after all the sailing I'd done, I assumed it would be an easy ride. I might even sock away a little more money.

Little did I know that John and two others would be dead in a matter of weeks, and my life would be changed forever.

two

The Wreck of the *Trashman*

From the moment I met John, I knew something was wrong. It was as if there were two people living inside me, and one was seeing all the signs, while the other was blithely plunging ahead. The acute senses I'd developed through years of dealing with crazy, dangerous people were picking up signals, setting off alarms. But I had learned early in life that if I just put on a confident face, I could deal with anything. I wouldn't see all this clearly until much later. But it was as if the dark force inside me, bred over a lifetime of calamity, was propelling me toward this ultimate test.

John was a skinny, weathered young man in his early thirties, with a scraggly moustache and a nervous squint. The first morning we met, I noticed that he was drinking Heinekens one after another out of a cooler, as he piloted a dinghy out to the boat we would deliver: *Trashman*. The name was appropriate. Once on board, I discovered the crew quarters and galley in chaos, as if a frat party had been going on there for a week. Empty Heineken bottles were everywhere, along with dirty dishes and rotting food. Sails, lines, tools, and other equipment were thrown in every corner. The beds hadn't been made, and dirty clothes and more empty bottles were strewn around in haphazard profusion.

The first morning that I officially went to work for John, he didn't show up at all. I managed to get someone to take me out to the boat and found him fully dressed on his bunk, passed out from drink. He took me back to shore, and we spent the day going from one bar to another. His style was a far cry from that of the focused, disciplined sailors I'd raced with. But his behavior and the chaotic condition of the boat, which might have caused another sailor to run screaming from the scene, had an odd familiarity for me: I'd been with people who drank until they passed out all my life, including my mother and more than a few of her husbands. But I didn't make that connection until years later.

By the time we left Bar Harbor, it was already late September, and John seemed reluctant to raise the sails, electing instead to motor to Camden, then Portland, then Falmouth Foreside, where his mother lived. There his girlfriend, Meg Mooney, came on board, and John proceeded to delay our departure once again. It was getting late in the season to make the trip, the days were getting colder and shorter, and the chance of big storms was rising.

As soon as Meg came on board, she and John began fighting. We spent our days going from bar to bar. On the one day that John decided to sail the boat, actually putting up the sails instead of using the motor, I found that *Trashman* wouldn't come about for our return trip, and John had to run the engine to get us back into the harbor. He hadn't put the centerboard down. In short, he didn't know how to sail. In addition, the boat wasn't in very good condition. The rigging wasn't tuned properly, and some of the lines were old and worn. The engine overheated and had to be shut down. John didn't seem to care.

Any one of these signs should have been enough, but I hung in there. I had learned too well the lessons of my youth and not well enough the lessons of the sea. For one thing, my mother and many others in my life were alcoholics. It was what I knew, familiar if not comforting. I had learned how to navigate around such people and survive. No doubt John's behavior fit with something in me. Although my experience at sea hadn't been very long, I'd been privileged to sail with some of the best in the world. I'd gone through bad weather and trying times, and I felt experienced. It didn't occur to me that I was putting my life on the line with this neglected boat and its incompetent captain.

During those days of waiting, lurching toward destiny, I was suppressing my own intuition and my awareness of myself and my surroundings. I was meeting what I call luck and timing, but both of those have a dark side as well: Chance can bring you luck that you need to recognize and take advantage of. But it can also bring danger. Only if you recognize it and acknowledge it can you adapt and avoid it. During that time, I really had a crippled will to live and vision of the future. I don't think it ever died in me, but I was at the end of a long, dark ride and didn't fully realize it. And I was not holding myself accountable for my own choices. I was simply moving ahead when my own intuition—my gut feelings about everything I was observing around me—told me to stop.

As the days wore on in Falmouth, I spent more and more time in bars. Sometimes I'd drink. Other times I'd gorge myself and end the day throwing up in the restroom. If this pattern of behavior didn't raise my alarm system, it's no wonder I was able to ignore all the other signs of impending disaster.

After two weeks, we finally left Falmouth for Newport, still without sufficient crew to make the trip to Florida. Meg had never been at sea, and the boat was more than John and I could handle alone. By the time we arrived, the Newport harbor was nearly empty—it was that late in the season, around October 14. And there the signs continued to mount up that this was a trip I should abandon. I ran into some people I knew in a restaurant, and they warned me about John's reputation. He'd had a lot of jobs, but none had lasted long. At that point I began to realize how reluctant I was to take this trip. My intuition was clamoring for my attention, telling me not to go.

Even so, I went with them when they left for Annapolis, still without crew. On the way, the weather turned, and John decided to head into Cape May, New Jersey, until it blew over. Again, he was unable to sail competently and had to turn on the engine, which overheated. Although the weather wasn't that bad, it seriously rattled John. It made me realize that not only did he not know how to sail, he didn't even like being on boats. And yet I stayed on.

⁂

From Annapolis, I called Sarah Cavanagh's mother to see if Sarah was available to make the trip. Fortunately for Sarah, she wasn't. Unfortunately for him, her brother Brad was. And once again, serendipity and synchronicity played a hand: I ran into Brad on the dock in Annapolis that very same day. He was with a Brit named Mark Adams, and both of them joined the crew on the spot. Brad was a competent sailor and a gentleman. But I didn't like Mark from the outset. He was a boorish, violent drunk and a liar. He claimed to be putting together a racing crew for a boat called *Ocean Greyhound* to sail the Sydney-to-Hobart race. But the owner had never heard of him, and the boat was in pieces. Mark was simply making it up.

My misgivings about Mark were bad enough that I told John I wouldn't go if Mark went. But John threatened me. He said if I left the crew, he'd make sure I never got on another boat again.

I called the owner of the *Trashman*, Morris Newberger, and told him that I was leaving the crew. But once I got him on the phone, I couldn't tell him the truth. Instead of explaining all the reasons for my decision, from John's incompetence to the boat's condition to inexperienced Meg and now Mad Mark, I simply said I'd changed my mind and wanted to go racing down south. He even asked me if there was something wrong with the crew, and I denied it.

In many ways, that was the end of my journey, the final destination of a lifetime of running. By essentially letting myself be bullied into going, I was giving up my inner self, giving over control of my life to someone, something, else. I abdicated my accountability, my vision of the future, even, perhaps, my will to live. I had hit bottom.

And yet in a way it was the perfect ending to that leg of my journey. I'd run so far from my crazy family I'd come full circle: This crazy crew was my new dysfunctional family. And like my mother, it offered the comfort of the familiar. Anyway, I had always been at my best in chaos, just like at age seven with a .357 Magnum stuck in my side by a man who was masturbating. I simply sank into the familiar flow of madness.

That last night in Annapolis, it was as if everyone knew the voyage was doomed. It was thick in the air. We drank the way people drank in my childhood—for oblivion—and Mark the most of all. We found him in a restaurant with a petite and pretty girl named Tilly. Mark stole a quart of Dewar's from behind the bar, and we went to continue the party on board *Trashman*. It was nearly dawn, and Mark was lurching around, drinking straight out of the bottle, when, on an impulse, he caught Tilly off guard, reached under her skirt, and pulled her panties down. Poor Tilly was so upset she immediately left, and the party broke up on a sour and shameful note.

We pushed off from Annapolis around noon in late October, battered, hung over, and exhausted before the journey even began. John had decided that we'd trade four-hour shifts at night. He and Mark would take the first shift, then Brad and I would relieve them, alternating until we reached Beaufort, North Carolina, where we planned to meet up with Tilly—if she was still speaking to any of us—for her birthday.

From there, we'd press on to Florida to deliver *Trashman* to its owner.

During that first night's watch, Brad and I began to form the bond that would ultimately help save our lives. Brad was easy to like, a big, gentle guy who knew and loved sailing.

On the morning of the second day, rising from my four hours of sleep at about eight a.m., I learned that John had either lost or forgotten some of his navigational charts, so we'd have to bypass Beaufort. The weather was good, and the reports that we received by fax promised more of the same. But by the afternoon, the wind had picked up; and by the time I took the four p.m. shift, it was blowing twenty-five to thirty knots under a darkening sky. By the end of Brad's and my shift, it had kicked up another five knots, and the waves were up to fifteen feet.

The rising winds and the demands of the boat did nothing to slow John's and Mark's drinking. If anything, they were drinking more. But John's behavior had changed in a curious way. He spent almost all his time down below instead of up on deck, often hiding in the engine room, tinkering with the engine while drinking a beer. It occurred to me that he was actually afraid to be on the ocean. That was not a comforting trait to discover in a sea captain.

The second night, the weather continued to deteriorate. John woke me during the four hours of sleep I was supposed to get. He was very upset about the weather. But when I went up to look, I didn't think it was that bad. I'd seen much worse and ridden it out.

But by the next time Brad and I woke to take the helm, the weather had taken a definite turn for the worse. The boat was becoming difficult to control. When I went to sleep after that shift, John soon woke me, again completely rattled. This time when Brad and I climbed up on deck, the wind was howling, and Mark was at the helm, howling drunk. When I saw him and realized our situation, I felt a sharp stab of adrenaline shoot through me. The seas, black and gleaming in the spooky sea-light of the storm, towered thirty-five feet into the air before detonating against the stern of the boat. The wind was up to fifty-five knots in gusts. Mark stood at an odd angle, small against this horrifying backdrop, and he was laughing, screaming, falling-down drunk. I heard Brad say, "Holy shit," as I moved to take the helm, and when Mark let go of it, he fell down and had to crawl across the deck before he disappeared below.

For the first time, I came face to face with the decisions I had made: This was the worst possible scenario for a sailor. The weather was fast changing from being just another bad storm to the worst weather I'd ever seen, even after spending an entire year at sea and going all the way around the globe. In addition, three out of five crew members were incapacitated. John and Mark were continuously drunk, and Meg came up on deck in the middle of the storm and was injured when she was thrown across the deck as the boat went into free fall down the back side of an enormous wave.

At the same time, the waves were literally tearing the boat apart. One came from behind and ripped the dinghy off the stern, taking the steel davits with it. I had never seen waves powerful enough to rip through steel, and it filled me with a pervasive dread.

By the end of the third night, Brad and I were exhausted and both very frankly afraid. The anemometer was hitting consistently near seventy knots, occasionally higher, and we were having real trouble controlling the boat. By four the next morning, we were in serious danger of losing our mast, Mark was passed out from drinking, and John was hiding in the engine room and refusing to come up.

As the day dawned, it became apparent how badly damaged the *Trashman* was already. I almost wished for darkness again so that I couldn't see the reality of what was happening to us. The wind seemed even fiercer in the daylight, as it blew the tops off forty-foot seas. The waves seemed to be coming at us from all directions. It was chaos, and it was getting more out of control. And here I was on a boat that didn't work with a captain who didn't know how to sail. I was more terrified than I had ever been, even in my childhood. At least then I could run and hide. Now there was nowhere to go.

After managing to get a couple of hours of sleep, I returned to the deck to find the anemometer gone, all the antennas ripped off, and the radar damaged. The engine had quit for good, and the centerboard was jammed halfway down. The cabin was completely trashed with chairs thrown everywhere and everything soaked and sloshing around. One of my watches with Brad dragged on to eight hours, as John and Mark lay incapacitated below.

When Mark finally woke up, he was crazier than ever. At one point, he tried to kill John with a winch handle; and he would have succeeded if Brad hadn't stopped him. Later on, he came lunging out onto the deck from below with a butcher knife in his teeth.

On that, the fourth day, John called the Coast Guard, gave them our position, and asked for assistance. "Charlestown Group Coast Guard," I heard him say into the microphone, "Charlestown Group Coast Guard, this is the *Trashman*, do you read me? Over."

"*Trashman*, Coast Guard Charlestown. Over."

"I think I'm going to have to ask for Coast Guard assistance," John said in a trembling voice. "We're really getting battered out here. The hull's down in the water, and things really don't look too good, to be honest with you. Over."

An eerie feeling came over me as I listened to him. I could feel a physical chill run all over my skin, and my hair seemed to stand up across my arms and neck. I had never been on a boat that had requested assistance from the Coast Guard before. And his call brought the reality of our situation into sharp focus: The port side of the boat was completely submerged, windows and all. We were taking on water fast—lots of it. John had run the engine, overheated it, and we were unable to charge the batteries. The bilge pumps, working full time, would therefore soon quit. It no longer mattered that the ship and its crew had been inadequate from the start. No one wanted to admit what I could now clearly see: When the pumps quit, if not sooner, *Trashman* was going to sink.

At about eleven in the morning, we heard the faint mechanical hammering of a light twin-engine airplane. As we watched, it was as if the symbol of a cross had precipitated out of the very stuff of clouds: Fuselage and wings dipped down from the overcast sky, maneuvered above us briefly, then dissolved once again, leaving us to wonder if it was real or not. The plane reappeared briefly, and then it was gone, and the sound faded in the moaning of the wind.

John was on the radio again, and the Coast Guard was advising him that two commercial ships were heading toward our position from about five hours away. We were for all intents and purposes dead in the water, with no sail out and no engine. After eleven hours on deck, I figured there was nothing more I could do but sleep. We just had to stay afloat for five more hours. Then I'd wake up, a ship would be there, and I'd get off *Trashman* for the last time.

What I couldn't know, could not imagine, was that while Brad and I slept, Mark and John lashed the helm and left their posts on deck. It wasn't the lack of bilge pumps that doomed us. With no one at the controls, the boat was carried up a huge wave and fell off onto its side. With the impact against the surface of the sea, water came exploding through the windows. I was so far gone in sleep, so unconscious from exhaustion, that I hadn't even felt it. The next thing I knew, Brad was dragging me out of bed and into water that was filling the companionway. As I struggled toward the stairs, it was already up to my chest.

I had gone to sleep expecting to wake and find two ships there to rescue us. Now, as I looked around at the open, empty sea, I felt my legs give beneath me and a sickening rush of fear. Time slowed to a crawl as my adrenaline surged, speeding up all my responses to meet the emergency.

Joseph Conrad writes in his novel *Lord Jim*,

> There are many shades in the danger of adventures and gales, and it is only now and then that there appears on the face of facts a sinister violence of intention—that indefinable something which forces it upon him and the heart of a man, that this complication of accidents or these elemental furies are coming at him with a purpose of malice, with a strength beyond control, with an unbridled cruelty that means to tear out of him his hope and fear, the pain of his fatigue and the longing for rest: which means to smash, to destroy, to annihilate all he has seen, known, loved, enjoyed, or hated; all that is priceless and necessary—the sunshine, the memories, the future; which means to sweep the whole precious world utterly away from his sight by the simple and appalling act of taking his life.

That was precisely how I felt when I looked out at the chaotic sea from the leaning deck of that vessel: That all at once, it was coming for me and that nothing could be more personal than its wrath. I saw that we must immediately abandon ship.

Meg was screaming as a wave threw her into the wire rigging of the main mast, tearing off her sweatpants and slashing her flesh to the bone. There was blood in the water as I swam away. Looking back, I saw Meg pick herself up, and she was immediately thrown back into the rigging again. Her screams reached me over the waves and roaring wind, and I shouted for her to try to swim in the lull between the waves. I watched as she again staggered to her feet and was thrown once more into the wires. I couldn't let her be killed right before my eyes. I swam back to get her off the sinking ship.

In the meantime, Brad had gotten the Zodiac, an eleven-by-five-foot inflatable dinghy, in the water, and the wind had promptly overturned it. Mark had hold of the life raft with all its supplies. And now my vision narrowed as I watched him in horror: The worst person in the world had hold of our most important possession, the only thing standing between us and certain death. The life raft canister contained not only the raft but also all the survival supplies—food, water, shelter, medicine, signal flares—that we would need in the days to come.

But Mark was in a panic, not thinking. And, as I watched, he inflated the raft before anchoring it to the ship. Numb with fear, I saw the raft blossom into a great dark kite for a moment. Then the wind picked it up and sent it bouncing over the waves. At first, Mark held on, and was dragged along with it like a rag doll. Then he let go, and our raft, our supplies, the one thread that might still have tethered us to life, were all gone.

We had somehow managed to reach the inverted Zodiac and were hanging onto the line that went around the outside, riding the mountainous waves in the screaming wind. It was all I could do to hold on, while Mark and John both screamed that we were all going to die. As we rose to the top of a giant wave, I saw the twin masts of *Trashman* as they sank into the sea and disappeared.

I was overcome by a sense of how unreal it felt. I wondered if this was really happening. Time had seemed to slow, and yet it had all gone by so fast. How had I gotten here?

Step by step, that's how. Although I wouldn't realize it until years later, I had been moving toward this my whole life, or toward some other calamity that would make everything else stop and force me to examine what I was doing and how and why. I couldn't know then that this was my transforming experience. All I knew at that moment was that my senses had become exceptionally sharp, even as I'd come to possess a keen ability to block things out. Mark's screaming became muffled, far away, while the taste of salt, the smell of rubber, and the warmth of the water became incredibly vivid.

They had prepared badly, drinking and dehydrating themselves with alcohol. They began their survival voyage at a huge disadvantage. Far in the background of my consciousness, I heard Mark screaming, "We're all gonna fuckin' die!" He was partly right.

Then began the long torture of fighting the waves. We'd be dragged up a wave, then thrown into a valley. Out of nowhere, another wave would crash down on us, wrenching the rope from our hands and pinning us under water. Or the wind would suddenly snatch the Zodiac and carry it away, forcing us all to swim for it. Rising and falling, flipping and swimming, we gradually exhausted ourselves. My legs began cramping, my arms were limp with exertion, my hands burned from the rope. We were being drowned.

On and on we rode into the night, hanging onto the outside of the Zodiac, getting under it, and trying various ways of keeping warm. I knew that hypothermia was our biggest immediate enemy. The water was warm but not warm enough. And the air was downright cold. Even in eighty-five-degree water, the body will lose one degree every hour during the night, and air temperature in the eighties will feel freezing cold. Losing only five degrees of body temperature causes apathy, slurred speech, and even amnesia.

It was then that we discovered that we had attracted sharks and that they were swimming all around us and even beginning to bump, which they do prior to attacking. Mark had begun complaining that I was kicking him, so I put my head under water to see what he was feeling. There were hundreds of sharks schooling around us, and a new wave of fear shot through me.

Very quickly, the boat was upright and we were all in it, cold or no cold. Hypothermia wouldn't matter if we were eaten by sharks. And since our supplies had blown away with the life raft, without water we would likely be dead in a few days anyway.

After years of running on my aimless path, I was suddenly faced with a situation that demanded I give everything I had. All the experiences of my life, all the learning good and bad, were about to be put to use.

By that time, I had seen how gravely Meg had been injured. Her leg and torso had been horribly slashed by the rigging wires as wave after wave had thrown her about before the boat sank. I had seen the way Mark and John had panicked during the sinking, how calmly Brad had gone about the work of detaching the Zodiac, how Mark had lost the life raft in his hysteria. But even before the sinking, I had formed my own ideas about what these people were made of and who I could depend on.

Even though I was sometimes gripped by debilitating terror—when I saw the sharks, for example—I was still able to return to reason. Meg was probably going to die without immediate medical care, which obviously wasn't coming. As for John, he should never have brought Meg, who knew nothing about the sea and its perils. She trusted him, and it was about to cost her her life. John knew that. He was the captain. If he lived through this, his career was finished. No one would ever entrust a boat to him again. If he was thinking about these things at all, he might very well decide that he had little to live for. Mark was, as far as I could tell, a confirmed sociopath who had proven himself violent, unpredictable, and completely incompetent. He might do anything, but I didn't have much faith that anything he did would be useful to our survival. Anyway, after all their drinking, they'd begun with a serious deficit in terms of nutrition, hydration, and stamina. They wouldn't last long. As far as I was concerned, I was the only person I knew I could count on. I might be able to count on Brad, but I hadn't made up my mind yet.

By thinking this way, I was starting to bring together the tools of my survival, using intuition, perception, reason, and will to create choices for myself that I could stand behind. Many years later, I would find that I lived my life this way and that it filled me with what I call the grace of God. You don't have to believe in a traditional god or subscribe to any religion to feel it. It's a force within all of us. And if we pay attention and work hard to recognize it, it will be there when we need it most.

When we spotted the lights of a ship that first night, I began to understand the difference between my way of thinking and theirs. As the others cheered at what they saw as our good fortune, I remained silent. I understood that it was extremely unlikely that the Coast Guard or any other vessel would spot us. We were on our own. The light appeared and disappeared with each rolling wave and at last was gone. I knew I had to concentrate on survival, staying alive and staying sane, minute by minute. And even so, every minute was a life-and-death battle with fear, panic, despair. It would have been so easy to let go and descend into madness. But I prayed and prayed to God to give me the grace to hang on.

Brad seemed the steadiest of the others. John and Mark, however, veered from hysteria to despair; and, as I watched them letting their emotions run out of control, I had to fight to direct my own thoughts and control my own emotions. I tried to wall myself off from them, from my entire situation, to go inside myself and find what was there.

Viktor Frankl, Auschwitz survivor, writes that "Everything can be taken from a man but one thing… to choose one's attitude in any given set of circumstances, to choose one's own way." Lying there in that dinghy in the middle of the ocean, surrounded by sharks in the dead of night, tossed about in a raging hurricane, I realized that I had gotten where I was through choices I'd made. And my way, my choice of attitudes, was now to accept where I was, what had happened, and to exert control over what I could control and let go of what I could not.

One thing I could control was my own emotional state. I could conserve my energy for survival through prayer and focus. I had always believed in God, and many people in trouble pray even when they don't. Prayer focuses the mind and clarifies your intentions. I was not praying for God to rescue me. Instead I was focusing all my energies on myself and what I could do, not looking to the others or the outside world for rescue or help.

All my life I had struggled against being a victim: that's what all that running was about. And I was determined not to be one now. I couldn't see all this as clearly at the time, of course. And I had to constantly struggle to avoid falling into despair or panic or even bargaining with God and making promises I couldn't keep. Still, I kept getting back on top of the situation, mentally and emotionally, sitting still and praying to focus my mind, then trying to use whatever was around me for survival. Time would pass, and time alone would tell. In the meantime, I had a job to do. As long as I was breathing in and breathing out, no matter how bad things seemed, there would be one more thing I could do to help myself. That was my job.

For example, we were all shivering uncontrollably from the cold, and, at one point, I hit on the idea of gathering seaweed to help keep the wind off of us and slow the process of hypothermia. It was a simple, practical step, using the materials at hand. Serendipity had brought us into a bed of seaweed. By being aware and willing to adapt, I had made the connection: Like it or not, this is our world now. We are in it, and we need to use what we find here.

When we'd brought the seaweed on board, and I'd covered myself with it, I saw that it sustained a whole ecosystem of living things. I found it beautiful, uplifting, to see this miracle of life. And I know now that the ability to see beauty in the world, even in the worst circumstances, is one of the keys to survival. It is using awareness to find grace. Even in Auschwitz, Viktor Frankl found beauty, describing a fellow prisoner who urged everyone out of the hut after a long day of forced labor to look at a beautiful sunset. It is in this quest for the joy of grace that we ultimately find our own survival.

I've heard countless survivors say that in a situation like this, you either get organized or you die. I got organized in my own way by setting two goals for myself—two visions of the future on which to focus. The first was that I wanted to set things right with my mother. I didn't want to leave the story unfinished. All the years of trying to get to her and get away from her had left me with a terrible need to resolve it somehow, for better or worse. I had to get back to do that.

My second vision of the future was that I wanted to make the Coast Guard account for itself in leaving us to die. I was really angry at them for spotting us, marking our position, and then vanishing. And my anger gave me strength. Anger can be a form of grace, too. So I had this vision of the future: I would live long enough to wash up on some shore and march my ass into some Coast Guard office and say, "Where the hell were you?" I just wanted them to own up to being guilty. As long as you have a will to live and vision for the future, you have a path.

When we are pushed to our limits, we often find great resources inside of us when we pay attention. At times during my days on the open sea, I sought refuge in my memories and imagination. I visualized beautiful green fields, dogs barking, children playing on a swing set, a ball game, cars turning into driveways—anything normal and pleasant to let me escape the hell around me, if only for a few moments at a time. This let my brain work on something familiar and unthreatening in a situation where all that I knew of the world had been suddenly stripped away. In this way, too, at least briefly, I was able to put myself in a state of grace. It's an all-important state to strive for in a survival situation, a kind of emotional and spiritual balance, a place of calm in a storm, where you are in and out of your circumstances both at the same time. On the one hand, I knew the gravity of my situation: No help was on the way, and without water we would die. Those were the facts. On the other hand, my will to live and my vision of the future meant that I had to strive, to do everything in my power to continue experiencing the world, to struggle minute by minute and wring every last drop of joy and pain from life.

Part of having a vision of the future and finding grace involves getting out of yourself and surviving for someone else or something else. Often this begins with simple empathy, feeling something for another person. As we rode along on the sea swells, feeling the sharks scrape their rough skin along the bottom of the Zodiac, I felt for Meg, who had so unwittingly fallen into what was certain to be a death trap for her. I wondered what her childhood was like that she was drawn to John Lippoth and the lunatic crew of the *Trashman*.

Watching her whimper and try to sleep, I hoped she was thinking of home or having some good thoughts. I wished that I had the power to stop her suffering or help her in some way. And simply having those feelings for another person made me stronger. It made me a rescuer and not a victim, at least in my own mind.

At the same time, I saw in Brad a possible companion in my quest for grace and balance, for organizing the chaos and consolidating our will to survive. I had watched him in his attempts to rise above his situation, to move beyond his own emotional swings. I knew from working those impossibly long watches with him that he was smart and strong and sensitive. Now he was quiet, sitting on the gunwale to help steady the boat. I sensed that he was working in the same way I was, and that if we could pool our mental and emotional resources, we'd stand a better chance. In addition, I knew I had to be accountable for my choices. I had gotten Brad on the boat in the first place. I felt an obligation to try my best to help him now. Accountability, taking responsibility for yourself and your own choices, is an important element of survival.

At one point, I covered my head with the rubber spray curtain near the boat's bow just to get away from the situation for a moment and collect my thoughts. I needed not to see Mark and John and Meg. On a moment's inspiration, I called Brad, and he came under the spray curtain with me. I proposed to him that we make a bond and help each other. I sensed that we both knew that the other three were at best useless, at worst, doomed. I suggested that we take turns sleeping and guarding each other. Just like many other crews who have been cast away through history and survived the impossible, we were setting up normal watches as if on a real boat. It was simple, organized, purposeful behavior using what we had at hand: Our own willpower and intelligence. And, for the first time, we had clearly drawn a line defining ourselves as survivors, not victims. It gave us a short-term goal that was attainable, and it gave us someone else to whom we were responsible. The person standing watch had a tangible future to look forward to: Sleep. And the person sleeping could sleep more peacefully knowing that someone else was on watch.

With the strength of our bond, Brad and I were able to better withstand what was coming next: the ultimate deterioration of the others on the crew and their gut-wrenching deaths.

It was during my turn to sleep on the third evening that Brad woke me, sounding urgently concerned about something. I sat up, and Brad pointed. John and Mark were leaning out over the side, drinking seawater. I felt my heart fill with pity for them. They had discovered the emptiness at the inner core of their selves, the lack of hope, the inability to see what's possible, and they'd given up.

The sea has twice as much salt as the human body can tolerate. As it gets into your system, it causes your cells to explode. Your kidneys try to get rid of it, but they're quickly overwhelmed. And it causes global malfunctions of the neurons in the brain.

They were doomed. I knew they were going to die. I just didn't know yet how terrible their deaths would be.

In a way, I think seeing them give up strengthened my own resolve to hold on. Thirst begins as an urge, a need, a want, but after a while, it becomes an all-consuming passion, then an incandescent pain that begins in the nose and mouth and eyes and spreads to consume the whole body. Baked by the sun in the day, frozen by the withering wind and sea at night, parts of my body that once seemed to have no sensation at all now seemed capable of feeling the most exquisite pain. In that condition, it's easy to wish for death, to accept it not only as inevitable but as natural, appropriate, even desirable.

Yet I kept telling myself that I would not fall apart, no matter what. I prayed and prayed to the God I had always known was with me, watching over me. I tried to be careful about what I prayed for, careful not to make extravagant promises. And when the worst fears gripped me, when I thought I was losing my mind, I would say the Lord's Prayer over and over. As long as I could remember the words and say them, I felt, at least I knew I was still here.

Poisoning yourself with salt doesn't take long to have its effects. In the early afternoon of the next day, Mark's mind snapped. He began searching around in the bottom of the boat, saying he'd lost his cigarettes. He claimed that he'd just bought beer and cigarettes at a convenience store and somebody had stolen them. John was losing his mind at about the same rate. When Mark asked him if he wanted a cigarette, an utterly mad conversation ensued that only two people out of their minds could have had.

John said, "Sure, you got any?"

"Under the seaweed," Mark said.

"I got some sandwiches," John said. "You want one?"

Then John began searching through the seaweed, hollering, "Okay, where are they? I know they were here."

Mark screamed at me, "Where are my bloody fags? I know you took them." Then the two of them suddenly collapsed like marionettes with their strings cut, and they sat slumped in a daze.

Sometime after that I awoke, having fallen asleep. Everyone else was asleep, too. Then John woke and started talking with Meg about flying home on a plane after we were rescued, and, for a moment, it seemed that he had recovered his senses. But just as suddenly, his conversation veered off again into madness.

"I'm just going to go get the car," he told Meg. "We're just off Falmouth. I know right where the car is. I'll go get it. You guys bring the boat in and I'll get the car. Then we can unload." He sounded so reasonable I had to ask myself if he was right. Were we right off Falmouth? His mother lived there. Wait a minute—weren't we there days ago? The whole experience for days now had had such an air of unreality that it was very easy to begin believing that it wasn't real. I closed my eyes to focus my thoughts, and, when I opened them again, John was going over the side. I screamed at him, and he just said, "I'll be back in a few," as calmly as if he really were going to get the car. The sun was going down and the water was teeming with sharks. As John hung there on the side, I was overwhelmed with a sense of unreality. Brad and I tried to talk him out of it, but John responded by saying, "I can't take this anymore. I'm going to go get the car." And then he swam away.

As we watched John appearing and disappearing amid the swells, we heard his horrible screaming commence as the sharks attacked him. And then all was silent once more. Meg began weeping pathetically. Mark didn't even react.

But then I collapsed too, and began weeping uncontrollably. I could feel the panic, the insanity, like a flame flickering just beneath the surface, my eyes darting everywhere, unable to focus on anything, my ears filled with his screams, my hair standing on end, and my skin burning and cold at the same time. I felt that my mind, too, would snap at any moment, and I had to quickly take back control, I knew, to prevent myself from following him into the water to silence his screams, which still echoed in my head. I began saying the Lord's Prayer over and over, rapid-fire at first, then gradually slowing, and it eventually began to steady me and drown out the screaming.

Later that night, Mark followed John into oblivion. First, in an obviously delusional state, he tried to have sex with Meg. When she began whimpering, he flew into a rage, screaming, "Fuck you. Fuck you. I'm tired of playing games. I'm going back to the 7-Eleven to get some cigarettes." Then he, too, went over the side. He moved hand over hand toward the bow and then disappeared.

A stillness settled over the boat and seemed to spread out to include the entire ocean. Then it was as if the world had exploded. Something rammed the Zodiac from below and spun it completely around. It felt like we'd been in a car wreck. Another solid blow, another spin, and the bow lifted high out of the water and crashed back down. Brad and I threw ourselves to the bottom of the boat and cowered there, holding each other, trembling and praying. We knew what was happening: The sharks were eating Mark beneath the boat and would soon tear the Zodiac apart to get at us. I tried hard to concentrate on my praying, to keep control, but a thousand thoughts were rocketing through my brain, propelled by fear—not only of the sharks, of death, but of my own looming insanity. I had looked insanity in the eye, first with John, then with Mark, and I knew how real and close it was, how easy it would be to let go and be swallowed up by it. I began to have dangerous thoughts: Why not just jump in and get it over with? What's the point of holding out and suffering? You're going to die anyway.

But at the same time I felt a deep sadness at the thought that I'd come this far, struggled so hard, and it would all be for nothing, that no one would ever know. After years of running and searching, I had at last glimpsed something within myself that had given me hope. I had seen my own strength and worth. I couldn't let all that go to waste. Yes, I had to answer for my past, but I also had to answer to the future.

Even as I had these thoughts, I realized that the worst was over. John and Mark were gone, God help them. Meg would die soon, of that I was sure. Then Brad and I would concentrate on survival with no distractions. For even while empathy is necessary for survival—empathy and a connection to someone and something outside you—there is also a cold determination in a true will to live. And it will reject those things—and even those people—that stand in the way.

In *Life of Pi*, Yann Martel writes, "When your own life is threatened, your sense of empathy is blunted by a terrible, selfish hunger for survival." And when mountain climber Joe Simpson broke his leg, his climbing partner Simon Yates tried at first to lower him down the mountain on a rope. But when Simpson slipped over a cliff and Yates could no longer hold him, he cut the rope. Even though he believed that by doing so he had killed his friend (he hadn't, and both men survived), he felt good that he had the presence of mind to cut the rope. Similarly, with Mark and John dead, although I felt regret for their fate, I felt stronger inside myself: I had cut the rope.

As I prayed and prayed that night, as the sharks gradually settled down to their occasional bumping and rubbing of the boat, I slowly realized that I was not going to die. I knew that I would do whatever was necessary, but I was not going to give up and die. The weather had cleared at last, and the stars were splashed brilliantly across the sky from pole to pole. I could see the Milky Way like a great smoky arch, and I could imagine our place in it, all these lives, all this joy and all this pain crammed into this tiny space in the vastness of that sky. And I told myself to focus on the sky, on the beauty there. At last, I fell asleep in the bottom of the boat, wallowing in the urine and seawater and the pus from Meg's oozing wounds, yet secure in the knowledge that I would live, no matter what.

Survival is a spiritual journey, whether it's survival at sea or survival of cancer, divorce, business catastrophe, or whatever other adversity life throws at us. And every survivor has a moment of transcendence and enlightenment, a deep spiritual transformation, a revelation. It seems to me that I had been searching for that all my life, and that somehow the trajectory I was on had inexorably led me to that precise spot in the ocean.

My moment of transcendence came with Meg's death. Meg was lying quietly in the bottom of the boat in the middle of the night, and Brad and I were sleeping next to each other. I awoke with an amazing clarity of mind. It seemed somehow that I understood everything all at once.

Then Meg began mumbling, and her hands began fluttering in the air. She began speaking in tongues exactly the way it's described in the Bible. Meg seemed calm now, her voice a monotone, her words incomprehensible at first, as she carried on a conversation with another world, another being. I had seen this once before in a revival tent in Texas: a woman speak in tongues. And now I heard God's message say to me clearly: "I am taking three souls and leaving you to tell."

It was one of those moments in life that is so raw and so real and so *God*. I felt His presence all around me. It was as if I was suffused with light. I had made the leap of faith, become convinced that I would live, and now I was one with God. I don't know that everyone recognizes their moment when it comes, but this was my moment with my Maker. I became one with that Entity. I felt It, I breathed It, I saw and heard God speaking to me through Meg, and I realized that I'd been on a quest to feel this all my life. It was euphoric. Every so often I still get a glimpse of it, even today.

Nietzsche said, "He who has a *why* to live for can bear with almost any *how*," and now I had my why. That ecstatic experience of God's presence in the world gave me a reason for living.

And the next day, a Russian ship picked us up 290 miles off of Kitty Hawk and the Cape Hatteras seashore.

three

Routine Miracles

Richard Feynman was the only physicist since Einstein who was widely regarded as a genius by his peers. In 1964, he was giving a lecture at Cornell University, trying to explain how light and electrons can be both particles and waves at the same time, and he said, "They behave in their own inimitable way, which technically could be called a quantum mechanical way. They behave in a way that is like nothing that you have ever seen before. Your experience... is incomplete."

And that's what I felt sometimes when I'd talk to people after the wreck of the *Trashman*: Your experience is incomplete. I wish I could put my eyes in your head so that you could see what I've seen. I wish I could put my heart in your chest, so that you could feel what it felt like to be on the ocean in that dinghy—just for five minutes, not for the five days that I endured. The abject terror, the constant physical suffering, the astounding closeness of death, and the even more astounding and intimate presence of God that comes with the certainty that you are going to live—live! I'd like to give you all those rare and precious experiences before you face your own sinking ship. Because to one extent or another, everyone faces that moment when you're called on to account for all the preparation or lack of it, when all your spiritual and emotional resources will be required, when you find out what you're really made of and what you're made for. I'd like to give you at least a taste of that before you need it.

My dear friend Nancy Russell was diagnosed with breast cancer in November 2000; as I write this, she is just finishing what we hope will be the last of her surgery. In talking to her, I can see that she used the same tools I used to save my life. We hear so much about breast cancer these days that those of us who haven't experienced it begin to think of it like having a fender bender. Well, our experience is incomplete. It's far more like being cast away into a sea full of sharks, watching others die around you and wondering if you're going to make it out alive.

The lump in Nancy's left breast was picked up on a routine mammogram. Nancy first had a lumpectomy, then radiation for seven weeks, and, almost exactly two years later, she was diagnosed again with breast cancer in almost the same spot. She decided on her own to have a bilateral mastectomy and then began the long process of rehabilitation, reconstruction, and recovery. Luckily, her lymph nodes were clear of cancer. And now, three years later, her attitude toward what she's been through—and toward her life in general—typifies what I think of as a survivor's attitude.

"It's been a rewarding process in so many ways," she told me recently, "because I look at life so differently now. When you're faced with the revelation of having an illness that could kill you, you start thinking about life as being more precious. The things you thought were so big are minute in the scheme of things. You no longer care about the new dress for the party or what people think. It no longer matters what you have or what kind of house you live in or what kind of car you drive.

"You go out of this world the same way you came in: With nothing but the people you love. Devastating circumstances make you look at life that way. That's true no matter what you go through, whether it's divorce or illness or something else. Now I try to be passionate in everything I do." Nancy, who's now forty-nine, devotes her life to charity work, especially raising money for cancer research.

What helped bring Nancy back from the brink? She talked of her very special group of "gal pals," as she put it. "We call it our Big Chill group." Some of them had known each since kindergarten. "I'm a latecomer," she says. "I came in fifth grade, moving from west Texas to Fort Worth. We just have a wonderful connection." And that connection is something she wanted to get back to while she was going through her survival journey. She wanted to live for herself, realize her own passion for life, but she also wanted to be in that relationship with those women who were so important to her. They acted as her support group during her illness. And in fact, clinical studies have shown that women who have a support group survive at a much higher rate than women who don't.

What did those other women do for Nancy? "We'd laugh, we'd cry, we'd get on each other's nerves," Nancy says. "But there's this wonderful bond there that I just feel very connected to." That group of women formed Nancy's vision of the future. "I had the will to live and the instinct to survive."

Nancy exemplifies another characteristic of survivors: She survived through helping someone else. "Every day that I went through radiation and watched other people going through it, whether it was brain cancer or little children hugging a teddy bear with a bald head and their mother crying outside, I sat up on that table and said prayers for those people, not for myself. I was one of the lucky ones—the lucky sperm club, as I call it. It was so tragic to watch all those other people every day, and I tried to combat that, not only with prayer but by trying to keep other people in good spirits to get their minds off it just for a few minutes. And I'd come away from there saying: I am blessed."

That ability to feel lucky in the midst of calamity is another characteristic of survivors. As I write this, there are people all across the Gulf Coast who are refusing to be victims and are behaving and thinking like rescuers instead. People whose homes and livelihoods have been wiped out by Hurricane Katrina are helping others, pulling them out of their homes, feeding them, giving them medical care—and feeling lucky. This universal attitude of a survivor can help you rise above any catastrophe.

Nancy, like me, had had some experiences as a child that built up her survivor personality. When she was eight, she had a go-cart accident that took her into a barbed-wire fence and nearly severed her leg. She still carries huge scars from that. But it helped build her will to live, honed her skills in suffering well, and lent her patience and endurance in recovery—all vital for survival.

A year later, Nancy's parents divorced, and her father took her from the tiny town of Monahan, Texas, near Odessa, to Fort Worth. To Nancy, it seemed like New York City: "I hated it." But the hardest part was losing her mother. The idea that her mother had given her up was a devastating blow to Nancy's young mind and heart. Perhaps that shared experience is part of my bond with Nancy. "I was very bitter," Nancy told me. Then a few years later, she watched her mother die at a very young age.

"It's called life," Nancy says now of those harrowing events. "It happens to everybody."

Another thing Nancy and I had that helped us through our later hard times was someone to turn to. I had Grandmother Queenie. Nancy had Littie. Littie worked for the Russell family. She arrived at six a.m., fed the family, got the kids off to school, and then cleaned the house. In the evening, she fed the family, got the kids into bed, and then went home and took care of her own family. "She brought me home from the hospital when I was born," Nancy says. "Coming from a small town in west Texas, I remember all the racism. But Littie taught me how important loving one another is. She taught me so much about loving and living and acceptance. She taught me about survival and how to hold your head up and carry on. She taught by example, and my father did, too. She was always there for me. And when we moved, she uprooted her whole family and moved to Fort Worth. Now she's in her eighties, and we're still just as close. I don't know what I would have done without her. She truly is my mother."

The human heart is a powerful organ of survival.

Here's the thing most people don't understand until they've gone through it: Every experience of survival is simply preparation for the next journey.

My friend Dashelle, a successful model for Neiman Marcus, was riding down a two-lane road, her friend driving, as they towed a horse trailer to Texas A&M. Coming around a curve, they were faced with an eighteen-wheeler coming at them, already sideways and jack-knifed, going fifty-five miles an hour. They met head on at a combined speed of more than a hundred miles an hour.

Dashelle was thrown through the windshield as the truck rolled over them. Her friend was killed instantly, and Dashelle was nearly dead when she reached the hospital. They had had to cut her out of the wreckage. Her life was changed forever. And yet she not only recovered, she thrived, looking back on the experience as the treasured suffering that made her who she is today.

Whatever form it takes, that eighteen-wheeler is always waiting around the corner to shape and reshape our lives. The challenge in such situations is not to fix blame for what happens to us. It is to find meaning in it and make some use of it. To let it enrich us and to embrace the new person we become. That attitude, it turns out, is also the key to surviving in the midst of it.

The survival experience is lived at the peak, in the moment, with time eerily suspended, actions taken in a flash, fates quickly sealed. But the after part is dull and slow, and doesn't feel anything like that at all. And a lot of what's happening is beneath the surface, as your mind, body, and soul work to make the extraordinary thing that happened to you ordinary, routine, assimilated. Part of you. Unless this happens, you haven't really survived.

My first thought when the Russian freighter picked us up after the wreck of the *Trashman* was that the ordeal was over. I'd been rescued and given another chance at life. I even imagined that after what I'd been through, the reunion with my mother would at last give us the relationship I'd always dreamed of.

But what I didn't understand then was that I thought I was still the same old me, thinking the same old way. And that was no longer true. Something tremendous, terrible, wonderful, horrible, earth shattering, had happened to me. To think that I could just jump off that freighter and pick up the old threads where I'd left them (tangled as they were!) was to deny the enormity of what had happened to me. Instead, I had to go through what was possibly an even bigger ordeal: I had to completely readapt my ways of thinking, acting, and living in order to survive the rest of my life.

This is another characteristic I've found in every survivor I've talked to or read about: They look back on their experience, however horrible it was, as the most valuable one they've ever had. They recognize it as the platform for growth on which they've built a better life, one they could not otherwise have had. They would not have wished this experience on themselves. They don't wish to repeat it. And yet—they cherish it.

These experiences are all around us, big and small. But most of the time we simply fail to recognize them. Whenever I talk to people about the wreck of the *Trashman* and my survival, I can tell that they see it as a really exotic and improbable experience. Of course (they think) nothing like that's ever going to happen to me.

I'm sure all those people in New Orleans felt the same way before Katrina hit. The people on the *Titanic* felt the same way, too. The woman stepping into the shower in the morning doesn't expect to discover the lump that will change her life. The people going to work one bright sunny morning at the World Trade Center did not anticipate anything out of the ordinary. And my friend Jana Posey never imagined that she was going to face her own death one night when she decided to go skinny dipping on vacation at a fabulous Mexican resort.

Jana is a flight attendant with a master's degree in psychology. She was married and had a two-year-old daughter when, in June 1998, she decided to take advantage of her ability to fly free to go on vacation. It was her sister Leigh Ann's first anniversary, so the two couples went down to Mexico and checked into the largest all-inclusive resort in Cancun.

After a few days of lying in the sun, playing with the jet skis, and sampling the cuisine from the various restaurants on the property, the two couples decided to go for a moonlight dip in the bay behind the hotel. There were no waves here as there were on the ocean side, just clear perfect water, and the moon was full.

It was deserted when they reached the dock and stripped down to jump in. The bay was deep enough that they had to tread water, and the four spread out, laughing and taking in the beautiful night. Jana was farthest out when she heard the sound.

"They make this roaring hissing noise," Jana told me. "To me it was the loudest sound in the world." The others heard a splash and assumed Jana was just frolicking in the water when she suddenly vanished beneath the surface. But somehow Jana knew exactly what was happening. A saltwater crocodile, eight feet long, swam up behind her, turned sideways, and clamped her head in its jaws. The sudden pressure broke her right cheekbone and tore into her left ear. The back of Jana's head was in the croc's mouth, and her face was looking out. "I was conscious the whole time," she says. She knew what was happening as the crocodile pulled her beneath the surface and began rolling her over and over. "They don't eat you. They roll with you until you drown and then they put you in their nest to rot."

And something in Jana said, "No. No, this is not going to happen, not here, not now. I'm not going to die like this." And she fought. "It was the fight of my life. I clawed and kicked and tried to bite—I was determined to fight." Somehow, she freed herself and shot to the surface, screaming, her face streaming and slick with blood.

When the others saw her, they assumed it was a shark attack. Leigh Ann and Jana's husband, Jeff, rushed toward her, while Leigh Ann's husband, David, got up on the dock to search for an oar or anything with which to fight.

As Jana screamed, trying to move toward Leigh Ann, she heard the hissing roar again, and the crocodile shot through the water and nearly bit her right breast off.

At one point, it got her under the water, and she was able to free herself. As the crocodile went to the surface, she stayed down to keep away from its jaws. She stayed underwater, formulating a strategy. "I could look up and see the surface with the light coming down. And I could see it up there." She saw the huge dark shape of the crocodile searching for her, and the light of the full moon coming down through the water. The silt they'd stirred up during the fight made glowing cathedral rays. And it was beautiful. Determined but not panicked, Jana knew that she had to get up there and get on with it or give up and drown. And she wasn't giving up. "I knew I had to go toward its tail to avoid its mouth."

She shot to the surface and grabbed a breath, and then Leigh Ann and Jeff were there. "The crocodile heard me and came at me again." By that time, Leigh Ann and Jeff had hold of her arm and began trying to pull her to safety, as the crocodile clamped down on Jana's left hand and tore her thumb almost off. David had returned by then, and he was thrashing and yelling and trying to distract the animal. When Leigh Ann and Jeff finally managed to free Jana from the crocodile's jaws, it turned and attacked David, who fought furiously as Jana climbed onto the dock. "My thumb was hanging from a flap of skin, and I was holding it above my head to slow the bleeding," she says. In addition, the creature had clawed all the way through her back muscles during the fight.

Naked, covered with blood, her face and chest and arms and back shredded, Jana stumbled across the four-lane highway to the back of the hotel, where a group of housekeepers and waiters were waiting for a bus. They began screaming "*Crocodilia!*" They knew. In the background, she could hear her sister shrieking, "It's got David! It's got David!" The staff began to take off their shirts and wrap Jana's wounds as an ambulance was called.

In part, Jana credits her experience as a strong competitive swimmer with saving her life. "I was fit and not intimidated by water. Being an athlete saved my life," she says. "I was very aware that I could die. I was angry and determined that I would fight and never give up. And once I was out, I knew I was going to live. At that point, I was more concerned about David."

Jana received a great deal of emergency surgery before she returned to the States, where her surgery soon continued. She was tormented by that hauntingly beautiful image of the crocodile against the moonlight, her view from the bottom of the ocean, a view that could have been her last. "I'd wake up in a full-on panic attack, profuse sweating, heart racing, panic-terror." It was even more maddening for Jana, because with her training in psychology, she knew exactly what was happening. She had post-traumatic stress disorder. But no matter what she knew intellectually, she simply couldn't control her emotional response or put an end to the nightmares. She went to therapists, but that didn't help either.

"The only strategy I had was time and easing back into the normality of life, and acknowledging that every day I got a little better. My addiction to physical exercise made me feel a bit more control. It gave me a goal. I began to approach my recovery as an athletic event: Here's my future, let's get on with it. I approached it like training. Deal with the future, not with the past. I just decided that I was going to be really good at being able to run again."

And bit by bit, she grew stronger, both physically and mentally. Previously, Jana and Jeff had been trying to have another child but without luck. And now, when there wasn't a place on her body that Jeff could touch without causing her pain, she became pregnant—twelve weeks after the crocodile attack. In Jana's mind, this was a miracle: "It had been impossible for me to get pregnant for two and a half years, and now God or fate or life had given me something to focus on that was positive in my future rather than dwelling on this tragedy in my past. Pregnancy is a consuming event. You're hard wired to have that overtake your awareness. And here it was: this miracle."

Jana acknowledges that the experience changed her for the better. "Now I feel different: I feel different from others and different from who I was before. I have had that second chance, yes. But I have also been tested. I have been mentally and physically tested to the point that other people never experience, and I have passed. That's a weird sensation. People always want to know: What am I made of? Well, I know. Instead of feeling like a freak show, I'm proud of myself. I'm just fine. And I have such incredible empathy when I look at people who suffer—someone who loses a child to cancer—what's the big deal about me?

"That event is always with me. But time takes it out of focus, and other things are priorities now. I'm a single working mother who goes to Europe all the time, and it's time to raise these children now. I feel almost invincible. I feel strong. I feel like whatever life hands me, I can deal with it."

There are two questions that I am inevitably asked by anyone who knows my story. The first is: "How did you survive those five days, and what did you do different from the others that kept you alive?" Over the years, my answer has never changed: I survived by the grace of God. I survived because I got angry. Like Jana, I made up my mind I wasn't going to die, and then I did whatever it took to ensure that outcome. Never in my entire life had I been so sure of anything as I was on October 28, 1982, the day we were rescued. I knew beyond a shadow of a doubt that the spirit of God as it exists within us, that mystical unifying presence, is the most powerful force we as humans have at our disposal.

The second question people ask is, "How did you go about surviving the aftermath and putting your life back together?" And the answer to that is more complex, sometimes even seemingly paradoxical. It involves a creative and sometimes chaotic process that has allowed me to learn and grow from the experience, as well as to deal constructively, instead of destructively, with the demons when they haunt me. Sometimes it just involves the process of being still and waiting for the answer—or the calm—to come to you. Sometimes you just can't force it by will. You have to welcome it through willingness.

Friedrich Nietzsche writes, "That which doesn't kill me, makes me stronger." I lived that quote. I have been to the abyss, and I have fought my way out. I have learned to adapt to the ever-changing world around me, and to accept and honor the pain from my past for the valuable coping skills it has taught me.

Life is not about winning some survival contest, cheating death or tricking fate. It's about making the most of the time we have here on earth, savoring one moment at a time. It's about thriving, not merely surviving.

Darwin writes in *The Origin of Species* that "the vigorous, the healthy, and the happy survive and multiply." To a certain extent, that process is unique to each individual, in that we all deal with our trials and tribulations in different ways. But there are common themes, best practices, lessons we can all use. In Jana's nightmares, hundreds of crocodiles appeared, crawling around on the floor of her room. She dealt with that and her physical injuries a step at a time, working each day to improve by small increments. Escaping the crocodile was one kind of survival. But the bigger task is facing the rest of life after the crocodile.

Yann Martel puts it beautifully in his fable adventure, *Life of Pi*:

> I would have given up—if a voice hadn't made itself heard in my heart. The voice said, 'I will not die. I refuse it. I will make it through this nightmare. I will beat the odds, as great as they are. I have survived so far, miraculously. Now I will turn miracle into routine. The amazing will be seen every day...'

Jana and Nancy are among the friends I refer to as "routine miracles." They're people who've had extraordinary experiences and have taken their salvation, their power, from the simple stuff of daily life. I try to do the same.

The answer to the question of how I survived surviving—how I went on after being rescued—is that I learned, over time and through continued periods of suffering and struggle, to turn miracle into routine. The storm, the shipwreck, the five days at sea, were just the brief preface to the real survival journey ahead.

four

Surviving Survival

The day after the Russian freighter crew plucked me and Brad from the sea, they passed us to a Coast Guard cutter, and I thought that the whole tragic event had finally come to an end. Never had I been so wrong. After Brad and I had said the last of our goodbyes and thanked the Russians for their extraordinary kindness, several young Coast Guard cadets helped us board the cutter. As I looked around the ship, there was a distinct and morbid contrast between the inexperienced, fuzzy-faced cadets of the Coast Guard and the rugged, seafaring Russians who had saved us. A wave of panic washed over me. I wanted to get off the cutter immediately. I had already entrusted my life to the Coast Guard once and had almost lost it as a result.

I felt the urge to rush back aboard the Russian freighter, to my saviors who had been so kind, but I was too weak.

I sat there in the corner of the cutter's cabin and cried, aware of sailors staring at me. I felt like a caged animal. I was also disgusted and angry. These men were part of the bureaucracy I paid taxes to, the same bureaucracy that had sent a plane to mark our position and then left us for dead. A failure to render aid at sea is a violation of maritime law. It's the worst thing one sailor can do to another in need, and they, the U.S. Coast Guard, had done it to me—and were responsible for the death of three of our crew.

All this was going through my mind when I caught one of the young cadets gawking at me. But when I made eye contact with him, he looked away.

"So how long have you been with the Coast Guard?" I asked him. My first calm words since boarding the cutter startled him.

"Uh, just about seven months. I really like it. I never even saw the ocean before I signed on. I never thought stuff like this really happened; you know, like being lost at sea and stuff." He rambled on nervously until I cut him a sharp-edged look. His words were only fueling the fire that already raged in me. But anger was a luxury I couldn't afford just then. I had to preserve the little energy I had left.

I don't know how long the trip to shore took, but when we docked, the pier was swarming with media. We were told not to answer any questions; and, with that, we were rushed to Morehead City and Carteret General Hospital. I was taken to a sterile examination room, where a gaunt-faced, middle-aged Coast Guard officer began asking me pointed questions.

Instead of being nursed back to health from the brink of death, I was being treated like a criminal. My brain was barely able to make sense of what he was saying, but as the gist of it seeped through my exhaustion, I again could feel the anger begin to throb in my temples as my blood pressure rose.

"Where are the others?" the officer asked.

I answered him with a trembling voice. My teeth were sore from five days of chattering in the cold. "They're dead," I said. "John and Mark drank seawater and went over the side. Meg died in the dinghy of blood poisoning, and we put her body overboard."

"And how do you know they're dead?" he asked, as if perhaps I'd somehow abandoned three live people out there.

"Because I watched them die one by one while we waited for you guys to show up." I searched his eyes for some sign of compassion, but there was none.

"Look, young lady," he began, "there is no reason for the attitude. These are questions that will have to be answered now or later. So let's make it easier on everyone and get it over with. If the others are dead, then explain to me exactly how they died; and is there any possibility that they are still alive?" I had had enough. I'd just come back from the dead—I damn sure wasn't afraid of this stern-faced, over-starched Coast Guard bully.

"They were eaten by sharks, and Meg died of blood poisoning. Didn't you hear me the first time?"

"Are you sure that Meg was dead when you put her body overboard? How do you know that it was blood poisoning?" he pressed on.

I took a long, deep breath. This was reminding me of all the times I was badgered as a child for something I didn't do.

The Coast Guard had made a mistake, and now they were looking for a scapegoat. I wasn't about to take the heat for Meg's death.

"Fuck you! Don't even go there. If you're looking for someone to blame, look in the mirror. You guys flew out to get our position and said you were sending help. The reason they're dead is because you never showed!"

He looked up at the attending nurse, "Do you think that we could get something to sedate her so we can get some answers?"

"I don't need to be sedated. I'm just fine, except for the fact that I just spent five days in a rubber dinghy freezing my ass off, watching three people die, while we waited for you guys to show up. Where's Brad? Get Brad. Brad!" I yelled. I looked the officer straight in the eye. "If you don't believe me, get Brad in here and see what he has to say."

The young male nurse soon returned with a syringe. But when our eyes connected, he knew all hell would break loose if he even got near me with that thing. So he diplomatically suggested to the Coast Guard officer, "Excuse me sir, maybe I can be of some help."

They moved to one side and had a whispered exchange out of my earshot. The officer then nodded, and the nurse came closer to the gurney and asked me, "Can you describe the condition of Meg's body before you put it over the side, any marks or discoloration, anything you can think of?" His eyes were kind, and he seemed to want to help bring this criminal interrogation to an end.

I closed my eyes to concentrate on the images that were still so fresh in my mind. Tears streamed down my cheeks as

I described the vicious nature of her wounds and the horrible condition of her body near the end. All of Meg's pain had become mine, and I couldn't help thinking that if only she'd just held on for a few more hours she, too, might have been here.

At some point during my description of her body, the young nurse stopped me and said I didn't need to continue. I looked up, and he, too, had tears in his eyes. He knew from my description how Meg must have suffered. He knew, too, that she was surely dead when we committed her body to the sea. He now turned to the rigid officer, spoke a few words, and, with that, the officer left the room mumbling about initiating a search for the bodies.

The young nurse returned to my side, holding out the syringe, and said, with a tentative air, "I know that you probably don't *need* this, but it might help with the pain."

He knew that aside from hypothermia and dehydration, my physical injuries were minor. My teeth had begun to chatter again, yet I didn't feel cold. My nerves were raw as my brain attempted to return to normal functioning after an assault that had put me only hours from death. How could he begin to know the psychic pain that made every inch of me feel like burned flesh? How could his medicine help me forget? I nodded for him to go ahead anyway.

As he withdrew the needle, I felt a numbing sensation spread throughout my body, throwing a blanket over my burning emotions. I was no longer in control. How weightless I felt as I let go at last. I felt Meg's ghost drift out the door with the nurse, and a moment later, our shared pain followed.

My days in Carteret General Hospital were hectic. I hadn't seen my mother in more than a year and had only talked to her once or twice in that time, but she suddenly became my spokesperson and publicist, basking in all the media attention. Before I had recovered enough to know what was happening, she had told the press that we'd decided to throw Meg's body overboard. It was the most insensitive thing I could imagine saying, given what Meg's family must have been going through, and it completely missed what an intensely delicate and empathic moment a burial at sea can be. I was furious that my mother was up to her old tricks again of vying for the limelight, and I forbid her to talk to the press. So she officiously busied herself screening my calls.

Everyone I'd ever known called. But one call that really mattered was from my Cochise. Even though our romantic interlude had been brief, we had gotten very close and were still extremely fond of each other. I can remember to this day the violent dreams he'd have of Vietnam, how he'd wake in a cold sweat, trembling all over. When he called me in the hospital, he told me in that serene way of his, "You have to be strong and feel the pain to put the pieces of your life back together." It would take me eighteen years to fully understand what he was talking about.

The day we left Carteret Hospital, Brad and I went to lunch with our families. Afterward, when the time came to say goodbye, we all drove to the harbor. Brad and I walked away from the group and stood looking out to sea. Somehow we couldn't fit in with those people, we couldn't yet return to the world. The salt air blew through our hair as we stood there without words, our bond holding us together like a gravitational field.

The sea was calm, and as I watched the small waves reflect the lowering sun, I wondered how something so beautiful, so placid, could become so deadly. How many sailors had the sea consumed? And how could the Coast Guard have forgotten us? All the self-pity I hadn't allowed myself to feel at the time came flooding in, threatening to drown me anew.

Standing there with Brad, I wondered how I could separate myself from someone with whom my life was so closely bonded. I felt empty and alone. It would be years before I read Viktor Frankl's account of his liberation from a concentration camp and came to recognize it in myself and so many other survivors I'd meet along the way: "We could not grasp the fact that freedom was ours," he writes. "We came to meadows full of flowers. We saw and realized that they were there, but we had no feelings about them... We did not yet belong to this world."

And neither did I. I had been to another world, and only part of me had returned. That's what Cochise was trying to tell me: That Mother Nature had spared his life, and mine, but that she kept a piece of our souls. Getting it back, becoming whole again, was the next—and perhaps much more demanding—journey. Jana had said the same thing. That in the immediate aftermath of her ordeal, she had felt freakish, out of place, apart, too different to take part in human activities. We all in our own way have to build our humanity piece by piece.

Brad and I said our perfunctory goodbyes, each deeply troubled. Then he walked away. As I watched him head back presumably to his home, his family, I suddenly realized that once again I had nowhere to go. My childhood home was long gone, and it had really only existed in my imagination anyway.

The home where I felt most peaceful was in nature, first with Grandmother Queenie and, for the past four years, on the sea. But Mother Nature commands respect, and I wasn't quite ready for her demands right now. So I flew back to New Orleans with another difficult and unpredictable mother—mine.

The plane ride numbed my body even as my brain burned with vivid, incoherent images. I shut my eyes and desperately scanned my life for a pleasant memory to cling to, but there were none. All I saw was pain. Cochise's words echoed in my head: "You have to be strong and feel the pain to put the pieces of life back together." But I just wasn't ready.

A sudden jolt of turbulence shook the plane, and I felt a rocket-rush of adrenaline surge through me. It felt as if someone was standing on my chest. I didn't have Jana's education in psychology so I didn't know that I was having a full-blown panic attack.

All of a sudden, I didn't know where I was. I'd gone so far into the past that I came up thinking I was still on the raft and had just been dreaming all this. I had escaped into memory so many times on the raft that I couldn't get my mind around the fact that I was no longer there. My eyes shot open and darted around the cabin of the plane to survey the situation, just as I had done in the dinghy. The dreams had seemed so real during my five days afloat that now I wondered if this might not be yet another one—a cruel, delusional dream of rescue from which I'd awake to find Meg dying beside me in a pool of pus and urine. I'd adapted so well to life on the raft that I was unprepared for this new reality. I could feel my mind stripping all its gears as it raced to fix on something familiar, but everything was too strange. It was as if some part of me still lived, could only live, on the raft, adrift at sea.

Another wave of turbulence shook the plane. A black spider of fear closed around my heart, and I could feel its venom surging through me. I desperately wanted the plane to land. I wanted to walk on dry land. I couldn't sit still. I wanted to scream, but I couldn't even draw a breath. I began to pray to calm myself as I'd done on the raft: "Our Father who art in Heaven, hallowed be… Please take this pain, please take this pain, please take this intense pain away from me—I can't take it anymore." Gripping the armrests of my seat, I silently begged for mercy.

On that plane, I remembered my old childhood prayer: "Dear God, I don't care how bad it gets while I'm young. I know I can take it now. But please, can I please be happy when I grow up?" There was a difference now, though, and I knew that I'd been wrong. I couldn't take it anymore.

When I was little, my Grandmother Queenie would hold me in her lap as I cried, gently rocking me back and forth, saying, "God never gives us more than we can bear. Someday it will all be okay, honey."

Now I felt like yelling, "But *when* will it all be okay? How much more do I have to endure before I can be happy? Just how much pain does happiness cost, God?"

The disordered chaos of my brain was screeching, and a cascade of images flowed out, completely out of control now. If there had been an open door, I'd have jumped out of the plane, but I was strapped into a seat, surrounded by people in an airless aluminum tube.

"Hold on. Just hold on," I muttered to myself. It could be worse, I thought. I could be dead. I could be the only one alive and still adrift in the Atlantic. But I'm not. I'm not a victim. I'm a survivor. I can live through this, too, I thought. And slowly, slowly, through prayer and focused meditation, I began to form a strategy: Think, I told myself sternly. Think: How did you do it at sea? How did you make it through the desperate, cold nights, sharks scraping their sandpaper hides against the dinghy, reminding us that we were nothing more than food? What did you do when they slammed into the dinghy and spun it around as they ate Mark beneath the water on that clear night? If you can survive that, you can survive this. It's just a plane ride, I told myself sternly. Even as one side of my brain seemed to go crazy, spewing images and noise, another side said: Choose life. That was death, and now that's over with. Now you have the miracle of another chance, another choice: Choose life.

And with that I suddenly relaxed. I had exerted control, just as I had in the raft. And I remembered this piece of advice I'd heard somewhere: "Choice, not chance, determines one's destiny." And I realized that when all the choices seem bad, just being still was the right choice.

When we reached New Orleans, it seemed that all I could do was lie in bed for days on end. My mother's home in the French Quarter was beautiful, but I was scarcely aware of it, focused as I was on my own interior landscape. All my waking thoughts and even my dreams were completely absorbed in trying to grasp the magnitude of what I had been through. Why did it happen? Was it bad karma? Paying for the sins of my parents? Was it random?

During those first days and nights at my mother's, I prayed and prayed: "Okay God, I give up. The joke's on me. What's the answer? Why me? Why are Brad and I still alive and the others dead? And just what am I supposed to do now?" But there was no answer.

From across the yawning void, I heard fragments of my mother's conversations in the other room: "I'm afraid that they missed something while she was in the hospital… She hasn't been out of bed in a week… Yes, she does have some wounds… No, no fever that I can tell… I would really appreciate that. Thank you so much. I'll look for you about four o'clock."

I heard her hang up the phone, then I heard her approach. "That was the doctor," she said. "He thinks it might be a good idea if he came by a little later just to check on you and see how you're doing. I think it's a great idea. You've been through a lot; and besides, you just don't seem like yourself."

That was my mother all over: She wouldn't admit that she was worried about me and wanted the family doctor to come and examine me. The way she'd said it made it seem as if it had been Dr. Wiley's idea, not hers.

I knew I didn't need a doctor. I needed a mother to hold me and tell me that everything was going to be alright and that we would get through this thing together, no matter how long it took. But the truth was that I already knew that time was running out. She couldn't stand to be around me for long, and soon I would again wear out my welcome. Doctors had always been a quick fix for Mother, and I knew that she needed to get me fixed up quick so that she could go on with her life.

"I'm going to the store," she then said, oblivious. "Is there anything you want?" She busied herself collecting my half-filled water glasses from the bedside table. I'd been obsessed with the miracle of having fresh water, as much as I wanted, but I could only drink half a glass. I'd save the rest, as if to reassure myself that there was more. Then I'd get a fresh glass and do the same with it. My mother took all my glasses and then left the room without waiting for an answer to her question.

Staying here wasn't going to help me get well, and I knew the time had come to get my ass out of the bed and do something. If I couldn't get God to come to me, then I would go to him. God helps those who help themselves, and He doesn't steer motionless ships. If I hurried, I could get to Saint Louis Cathedral and back before Dr. Wiley dropped by. I dressed and rushed outside.

As soon as the courtyard gate shut behind me, I was overwhelmed by the acuity of my senses. This was the first time I had been outside since I arrived in New Orleans, the first time I had been alone since our rescue. It felt so good just to be alive, to feel the breeze against my face. I felt the life in every hair on my body. But then anxiety made my chest so tight I could hardly draw a breath. The streets seemed to engulf me in a cacophony of sights, sounds, and smells. I felt trapped between heaven and hell—the miracle of being alive and the chaos of my disordered senses. In my confusion, I wondered for a moment if perhaps I had actually died with the others. Maybe this was Purgatory.

I stubbornly concentrated on putting one foot in front of the other, feeling every step as if it were my first. I walked to the end of the street and turned right. I hadn't been to the cathedral since I was a child, but my feet seemed to remember the way. Everything around me stood out in sharp relief like an overdeveloped Kodachrome. The trees and plants seemed to glow with a vibrant green energy. Every sound was crystal clear.

I wouldn't understand what I was going through until years later. It simply felt like I was on the verge of insanity. The people passing me on the street seemed foreign, as if they were from another planet, but familiar—it was a planet I'd been to. Was I on the outside looking in? Or was I on the inside looking out? Or was this just some stress-induced flashback from a past hallucinogenic experience? Whatever the case, I wasn't fitting into the picture. I felt like I was not really there or didn't belong there.

None of it made any sense. So I simply put one foot in front of the other as if walking a tightrope until I reached the imposing entrance to the church. For more than two centuries this church had been a haven for lost and abandoned souls. Maybe here I could find my soul again. There was no trace left of the young, adventurous spirit who had so loved living, hard as it had been. I stood there waiting for something—I don't know what. I wasn't Catholic; I wasn't really any religion. I had been raised around the Church of Christ in the Bible Belt of Texas, and had been baptized Episcopalian. But it didn't really matter, because the God I was looking for didn't care what religion I was.

During some of my worst years as a child, we would often visit family friends who lived in Wichita Falls. They had four children, all of whom were about my age. On some occasions I even got to spend the night. For me, those visits were a port in my unending storm. They lived in a big, beautiful home, always had the prettiest Christmas tree, and seemed to be the happiest people I'd ever known. They were Catholic, and I longed to be part of their Catholic family. I remember going with them to their mysterious masses—the robes, the incense, the chanting in Latin—and then watched the kids study their catechism lessons. They took it so seriously that I was convinced that somewhere in that religion lay the secret to happiness. I desperately wanted to share in that secret.

I pushed the massive door open and entered the vestibule. I crossed the tiles, my footsteps echoing in the empty church, and lit three votive candles, one each for Meg, John, and Mark. I knelt before the flickering lights and said a prayer and watched the candle flames tremble as I breathed in the still air. But I had carried that surreal, dreamlike feeling into the church with me. I wondered if my soul had actually departed with theirs to some distant place beyond this world, and if my body was left here walking the streets as a zombie—my punishment for living where they had died.

I stood up from the kneeler in front of the candles and moved deeper into the cathedral, smelling the musty odor of ancient stone and candle wax mixed with the faint scent of incense left over from High Mass. As I entered the sanctuary, I felt a chill spread over my body. I breathed in the smells, and with each breath, I could feel my chest opening, my shoulders dropping, my muscles relaxing, until finally, a great rush of sadness seemed to pour forth from deep within me, and I began to cry. As I gave in to the feelings, I sobbed uncontrollably, my cries echoing off the leaded glass and ancient tiles and high, arched roof beams. And as I let the venom that had raced through my veins for days pour out of me, I began to feel a calm enter me in its place.

The slight touch of a hand startled me back to reality. My response was all out of proportion: I went into a full panic, every hair on my neck and arms seeming to stand upright like St. Elmo's Fire, as the fear gripped me once again.

"Are you alright?" asked a kind-looking, middle-aged woman.

"Oh, I'm fine, thank you." The words were a protective shield, a reflex from years of training: Never show weakness.

She left, and I was alone again, wishing I could have told her everything. But somehow I now felt calmer, more familiar to myself. It was as if a fragment of my soul had moved back into me and filled the vacant space. I tried to retrieve my pain. I wanted to feel it again, but it had been numbed. I was numb. Emotionless. Then, from somewhere inside me, *It* spoke:

"God is here, but I don't think He wants to talk to you right now. Besides, you really need to pull it together. All this pissing and moaning isn't going to get you anywhere. Remember: God doesn't steer motionless ships. You've got a lot of work to do if you're going to get through this, so you'd better get off your butt and quit feeling sorry for yourself."

I had thought for sure *It* was gone—that the sinking had been more than even *It* could endure. Now, I wanted to send *It* away, but I knew *It* wouldn't go. I had grown comfortable in my self-pity, but comfort had never been on *Its* agenda. *It* came when I was little girl and taught me how to read and assess situations from a distance to avoid danger. *It* taught me to control my fear and focus on the here and now. I didn't always heed *Its* warnings, but *It* always kept them coming. *It* was cunning, intuitive, and brave, and had little patience for my self-pity. Although no one "knew" *It*, almost everyone who knew me sensed *Its* presence. Over the years, my friends came to refer to *It* as The Wolf.

"Get off your butt and quit feeling sorry for yourself," The Wolf had said. But I wasn't sure I had the energy to keep on living. And even if I did have the energy, I wasn't sure that living was worth the trouble anymore. There were so many obstacles to deal with—memories, death, bulimia, Mother.

I began to pray: "Dear God, I know that adversity makes you stronger. But I don't want to be any stronger. I'm tired of being strong. Look at the mess my life is in. God, I know You can't put the pieces back together for me, but I don't think I can do it by myself. I need your help. Please, dear God, show me how to put the pieces back together." Then I waited for an answer, a sign—anything. But nothing came. I was simply a twenty-four-year-old girl, alone in an old building in New Orleans.

All the time I was in the water, I had had a vision of the future that kept my will to live strong. I had my reunion with my mother. I had revenge against the Coast Guard. I had the determination to survive this and get to land and live on. I wanted to make it all mean something, to be able to tell my story to help others. Now I had seen that there was no revenge against the Coast Guard. There was going to be no relationship with my mother. I could find no meaning in the pointless loss of life and in my random survival. I'd been cast up on land, but it felt as if what was cast up was a shell with nothing in it. What now?

The maddening thing was that God had spoken to me on the dinghy in Meg's dying words. Call it a physiological response to a dying brain, call it hallucination—it doesn't matter. The impact on me was the same. God told me, "I am here for you now, as I have always been and always will be." So where was He now and why wouldn't He talk to me?

"Hey! Remember me, God?" my mind screamed. "The one in the life raft? Well, I'm in church, God—where are you?"

In the silence that followed my angry outburst, I could again hear Meg speaking in tongues, the voice of God reaching me at my darkest moment, and I remembered that feeling of oneness. I'd been so close to death, yet so full of life. It was a moment of grace.

I sat forward in the pew, suddenly alert: Grace, I thought. That was it. That was my gift from God. He'd heard my prayers, spoken to me, and then I'd been rescued. My prayers *had* been answered. He had heard me and spared me, and now it was my job to cherish my most precious divine gift of life.

The Wolf was right: God was here, waiting and watching; and I had to get off my butt, because now the ball was in my court. Instead of sitting here feeling sorry for myself, I had to keep my miracle, my divine gift from God, alive. Because God doesn't simply come down and lift our burden, relieve our suffering. Sometimes, in fact, the gift he gives us *is* our suffering. Sometimes our most important job is to learn to suffer well and find meaning in it.

I took a deep breath to compose myself. The warm energy of the church filled my lungs and gave me new hope. I was the unlikely recipient of a miracle, and now I felt a strong obligation to live the part: To be accountable. I just hoped I had it in me. Somewhere in my head I heard Grandmother Queenie's words: "God never gives us more than we can bear."

I lifted my wrist to see the time and realized that I didn't have a watch: It had gone down with the *Trashman*. Once again, I felt panic grip me. Mother hadn't been home when I left, and I hadn't even written a note telling her where I was going. If Dr. Wiley got there before I got back, I knew my mother was fully capable of throwing me out of her house in one of her capricious overreactions. I'd have nowhere to go. I rose as quietly as I could, made my way to the end of the pew, genuflected, crossed myself, and hurried out of the church.

I ran all the way home. I had to start getting my life in order. I had to begin the process of exorcising the demons I'd brought home from the sea. I began talking to myself as I ran: What is the biggest immediate threat to my well-being? The sinking? Yes, because the memories are making me feel that I'm losing my mind. But no. I was rescued. That danger is in the past.

My mother? Yes. She's always driven me crazy. Besides, she may very likely kick me out when I get back, and I'll be homeless and on the streets. But no. That's been going on all my life, and I haven't gone insane yet. As for being homeless, I can certainly survive the streets of New Orleans.

Bulimia? Yes. It depletes my body of valuable nutrients and electrolytes and destroys the lining of my stomach. It makes me feel crazy, it threatens my sanity. It could very well kill me.

There it was, then. I knew the answer to my question. The most immediate threat was bulimia.

As I ran along the street, I heard The Wolf's voice in my head once more: "You knew the answer all along." My head filled with haunting images of the past eleven years of hiding in bathrooms, squatting over toilets, pouring my life into the sewers.

I felt like plugging my ears and yelling to drown out the truth of these words. The Wolf loved a worthy opponent and had challenged my obsession for years. Bulimia was a devastatingly destructive addiction that was destroying the precious body God had just saved.

I knew that I had to heal this one thing that had not only stolen my focus for more than a decade but which continued to threaten my life. I was scared to death of the idea of healing, yet energized by it at the same time. I had been baptized in the tempestuous waters of the Atlantic Ocean, and this was my new beginning. And that thought gave me strength. The Wolf and I were preparing to wage war on the demon that had possessed me for so many years.

Out of breath, I slid the key into the lock and opened the door to the courtyard. To my relief, Mother wasn't back yet. I ran up the stairs, drank another glass of precious water, and The Wolf and I crawled into bed to wait for Dr. Wiley's visit.

I'm floating in an inner tube. It ascends a great swell, and I'm able to look out over an endless sea of black carpet pulsating with huge pink-and-green cabbage roses. I know those roses, I think to myself… Where is that rose carpeting from…? The undulating movement is hypnotic. I want to rest here forever, but I know I must get up. I have to go somewhere; but the gentle yet sinister rocking motion is seductive and holds me captive. I struggle to move but have no control over my body.

It's so peaceful here, so beautiful. As I float over the top of the swell, moonbeams reach through the window to light my descent into the darkness of another trough between the great waves. Luminescent arms reach down to save me, but when I reach for them, they vanish, ghostly, into the clouds. I sink deeper into the abyss between waves. How did I get back in this ocean? Where's Brad? He said he wouldn't leave me here alone.

The cavernous trough stinks. I can hear a man crying, but it isn't Brad. It's so black out here. Where are you? Who are you? Please help me!

But it isn't me. I am some other girl.

Help us!

I feel the pain in her silence. So much pain. I want to get up and walk across the flowered carpet to her, but I can't move. I am paralyzed. I can't escape the floating cabbage roses.

The poor girl is so cold. I tell her without words, "When I was so cold in the dinghy, I peed, and it made me warmer. Try it. I promise, it helps."

I feel the dream let go.

I feel my bladder let go.

I should have known.

"No don't do it!" I yell at her. "It's a trick to make you pee in the bed. Don't do it! It's a dream! It's a dre—"

"Deb, Debbie. Honey. It's just a dream. Wake up." I felt my mother gently shake me as I rose from the haze of sleep. "Are you okay?" she asked with concern.

"Yeah, I'm alright, but your bed isn't." I lifted the sheets. "I'm sorry, Mom."

"Another one of those dreams?" she asked.

I shrugged.

"Well, don't worry. We'll take care of it later. Wiley just got here, so why don't you just clean up a little and you can throw this robe of mine on." She laid the robe across the foot of the bed and started out of the room, "Don't take too long. We don't want to keep Wiley waiting."

After a few minutes, I emerged from her room completely humiliated by my inability to control the dreams. Dr. Wiley greeted me in his kind, attentive manner. He asked the usual questions with a few added comments about how lucky I was to be alive. He took my pulse, listened to my lungs, and then turned to my mother. "Everything seems to be fine physically, with the exception of those horrible saltwater sores and a few scratches and cuts. She's tough. But after her having gone through something like this, you may want to think about getting her a little help to get over some of the psychological hurdles. I'd be more than happy to give you the names of a few doctors who specialize in this kind of thing."

Then he turned to me. "Debbie, is there anything in particular that's bothering you?"

For a split second I wanted to pour my heart out to him. I wanted to know how to get over the bulimia, the dreams, the pain of living right now. But I was afraid of my mother. I knew she might throw a fit if I brought up the bulimia right now.

I thought back to Thanksgiving five years earlier, when Mother had been married to husband number five and living in Reno, Nevada. I had called to make my holiday plans, but she had snapped at me that I was too disruptive and would have to find somewhere else to go for the holidays. Then several days later, she called back all sweet and happy and sent me a plane ticket. I didn't know whether I was coming or going, and I felt like I was walking on eggshells the whole time I was there. We had an awkward Thanksgiving dinner, and a little later, I was in the bathroom, bent over the toilet getting rid of it when Mother walked in on me.

She asked if I was sick. All I could say as I sat back against the bathroom wall with tears rolling down my face and vomit in the back of my throat was, "Yeah, I'm really sick. I need help, professional help."

But when I told her that I was bulimic and had been for seven years, she dismissed it, saying it was just "growing pains," and that I'd get over it eventually. She refused to listen to me, no matter how much I pleaded for help. My story didn't fit with hers, and she wouldn't hear it.

Here with Dr. Wiley, the story line was not supposed to be about some long-standing eating disorder. My story was supposed to be about the sinking, the miraculous rescue, and everyone living happily ever after. My mother didn't want any complications to this neat conclusion. In her view, I'd been living a perfectly normal life, perhaps a bit spoiled, when I made this bad decision to get on a bad boat. Then the bad storm came and sank the boat, and I was severely punished. Then the good sailors came along and rescued me, and now I could live my life in a more normal manner, perhaps a bit chastened since I'd learned my lesson.

I'd always fit my story into hers, and there simply wasn't any room in her life for the real story of mine. My story didn't fit, so I simply pushed it away rather than risk her wrath. But to have no story means you have no life. You don't exist.

So I did exactly the same thing I'd done before getting on the *Trashman*. Just as I had lied to its owner about the fitness of the crew, now I lied to Dr. Wiley about my own fitness. I ignored my intuition and pushed away the one person who might have helped me at this moment. I doomed myself to yet another desperate voyage.

"Nothing really big, I guess," I lied. "Just the dreams. They just don't go away. I kind of know that they're dreams when I'm having them, but I can't seem to wake up in time."

"In time? In time for what?" he asked, seeming puzzled.

I hesitated. "In time for me not to urinate in the bed," I said sheepishly.

He sat quietly and thought for a moment. "Do you want to tell me about the dreams?" he asked.

"They're just floating dreams," I said. "I'm always in a big rubber inner tube just floating. Sometimes the surroundings are different, like this time the ocean wasn't water. It was carpet—this black carpet with green and pink cabbage roses floating everywhere."

Mother had a strange look on her face. "You know, the carpet in your bedroom on the ranch looked something like that."

And it hit me all of a sudden: That was the carpeting I'd stare at so intently when Mother's third husband would come into my room at night and lie in my bed masturbating with one hand while holding a loaded gun against my body with the other. To make this go away, to make him go away, *I* would go away: I would disappear into that carpeting as if I were floating away on the waves. The self that became no-self would float into that black sea of cabbage roses as I escaped the horror of what was really happening to me. And now I was escaping again in the exact same way. Of course, I said none of this.

Dr. Wiley was speaking again, and I tried to concentrate on what he was saying: "Well, I can't give you much advice on the dreams; but tomorrow I'll call with some names and numbers of a few colleagues I can refer you to in that field. I'm sure that they will be of more help with your dreams than I can be."

That was the answer, I was sure: Someone who would listen to my story. Between my childhood trauma and the shipwreck, between the bulimia and the dreams, I knew I needed to see a psychiatrist, and now I'd get to see one. Another prayer answered. I would exist again, because I'd tell my story to someone who wouldn't deny it. And, I reasoned, because it was Dr. Wiley's idea, Mom would have to believe that it was a good one. This looked like it might be the first step toward reclaiming my life. And what is a life but all the experiences we've had and the story we make out of those experiences and then share with those we love? For the first time in ages, I felt like things might just work out after all.

Later that evening, Mother and I went out to dinner, and we talked for hours. We even apologized to each other for some of our past differences. I thanked her for coming to Morehead City and bringing me back to New Orleans to recover. She said that she wouldn't have had it any other way. "I'm your mother," she said. "That's what mothers are for." I felt closer to her than I had in years.

That night, I lay in bed nurturing the hope that our dinner together, and the promise of professional help to come, had given me.

Maybe now, Mother would hear me. She'd realize my bulimia wasn't just "growing pains" and that I wasn't going to get over it without help. Surely she would understand, especially since she herself had been to several treatment centers since then to dry out and get help with her alcoholism. Surely that must have changed her story enough to make room for me and mine. I felt I had a real chance at last to see a psychiatrist. For the first time in weeks, I slept like a baby. No nightmares, no dreams, just blessed sleep.

The next morning was a beautiful autumn day, bright and crisp. A light rain had washed away the stench that always seemed to linger on the streets of the French Quarter. Still in our robes, Mother and I drank chicory coffee out on the terrace overlooking the street. Everything seemed so right and so in place.

"So, what are your plans for the day?" she asked.

"Not much really. I thought I would go down to Saint Louis Cathedral, light a few candles, and see if I can talk to the local spiritual demon-chaser—you know, to see if he has any advice on how to get rid of the dream demon. Maybe a quick exorcism or something."

"That actually sounds like a good idea. Lord knows, this is New Orleans; and if there's a good demon-chaser anywhere, he's bound to be here in the French Quarter. But you'd better call and make an appointment. He's probably booked from now to eternity."

We both laughed. It felt good. She seemed to be hearing me at last. Mother went inside and got a phone number. I made the call, and much to our surprise, I was able to get an appointment to see Father Vincent Verderame later that same morning. Everything seemed to be going my way.

On the walk through the French Quarter toward the cathedral my emotions were completely different from those of the day before. I was still strangely aware of my surroundings with that hyper-acuity that goes with responding to stress. But instead of feeling threatened by it, I was oddly comfortable. I was an observer. I felt confident enough to take a detour down Royal Street to St. Ann, which would take me right to Jackson Square and the cathedral but allow some sightseeing on the way.

I was amazed at how different the world looked since the sinking. As I stared into the windows of the trendy shops where I'd shopped in recent years, I wondered what people did with all the junk they bought. I suddenly saw how people were sold everything but what they needed. Thinking about that, I realized that almost everything I owned had gone down with *Trashman* and was resting on the bottom of the Atlantic Ocean. Besides the red Charles Heidsieck sweatshirt I was wearing when we sank—a memento from one of my buddies who sailed on the *Charles Heidsieck* during the Whitbread Around the World Race—all I had left to my name was a little cash in a bank account in Maine. The strangest thought came into my head: I had gotten that red sweatshirt from one of the guys during Whitbread. Then I had sailed with Brad's sister on the *Charles Heidsieck* and that was how I met Brad. That poor red sweatshirt was the connecting thread in all those events. For a brief moment I felt sorry for that sweatshirt; then I decided it was cursed and had to be thrown away—no, burned!—the minute I got back to Mother's. I started to laugh at my crazy thoughts. At least I was able to laugh. Humor is the great antidote to fear.

The narrow street was filled with constant motion, mimes and boys dancing and musicians playing, all soliciting tips from tourists. And watching them, I thought: All these people are doing is trying to survive, just like me. It was the first time I'd felt reconnected with the world.

When I arrived at Saint Louis Cathedral, I was a few minutes early, so I went into the vestibule, again lit three candles, and said a prayer. As I looked down, I noticed the donation box, which I hadn't seen the day before. I was embarrassed: I didn't even have money for the candles. I looked around and made a quick escape before anyone noticed.

When I was ushered into Father Verderame's office, he said, "Your name sounds vaguely familiar. Is there some reason that I should recognize it?"

"Well, you might have heard it on the news. There's been quite a lot of press about the accident."

"Are you the young girl who survived that shipwreck somewhere off the Carolinas?"

"Yes sir, that would be me." He motioned for me to sit down.

"What can I do for you, Debbie?"

"Father Verderame, I was hoping that you might know the answer to that question. I feel like I'm dead inside. My heart hurts so bad sometimes I wish I were dead. So much has happened—I just need to try and make sense of it all."

"Why don't you start from the beginning and tell me the story?" he said.

The beginning, I thought... If he only knew the true beginning some twenty-four years ago... I remembered the sea of cabbage roses on the black carpet and thought: That story would take days, weeks, maybe even months to tell. Maybe the rest of my life. Somewhere in the back of my mind, The Wolf cried out that yes, one day, I'd have to tell it. But I really wasn't ready after all. I pushed the voice away.

I reconnected my train of thought and began my story of the voyage of the *Trashman*, as the priest sat there and patiently listened, his eyes growing gradually wider and wider. When I had finished telling him about the sinking, the suffering, the deaths, the horror, he was silent for a moment, staring at me in quiet astonishment.

"That's quite a story, young lady." He stopped and thought a moment longer. "Can you tell me what it is, the one thing that bothers you the most about this tragic event?" he asked.

I had never really thought to divide it up into gradations of horror. It was a whole experience, and it was completely baffling, from the deepest terror and sorrow of my life to the ecstatic recognition of how beautiful the sea and sky could be on a clear night. It had contained all the elements of existence, all possible thoughts and emotions, jammed into the most intense five days of my life. If you tried to dissect it, it would evaporate like a cloud.

"The whole tragic event," I replied humbly. "It was my worst nightmare out there. I watched three people die, and yet I didn't die. And the truth is that I never thought I would die. I feel like I have been the unlikely recipient of a miracle. God saved me for some unknown reason, and I'm not sure what that reason is. Please don't get me wrong, Father Verderame. I don't think that I'm something special now, but I do think that it's my job to keep that miracle alive. When Meg was dying and spoke to me in tongues, I felt His presence. I felt one with Him and I want to feel like that again instead of feeling all this pain." I stopped and waited for something profound to come out of his mouth.

"Debbie, are you a Catholic?" he asked out of nowhere.

I was a bit taken aback. "No sir, I'm kind of a mixed breed." I wondered what being Catholic had to do with anything.

"Have you been baptized?" he asked next.

"Yes sir, I was baptized an Episcopalian when I was nine or ten."

"Well, I think that you need to become a Catholic. Archbishop Hannon will be here on December 5 to do confirmations. So we'll need to get to work if you're interested. Well?" He raised his brow and waited for an answer.

I couldn't even think. I had come for answers, not conversion. "Am I going to have to take confirmation lessons?" I asked, remembering how many hours my childhood friends had spent on their confirmation studies.

"Yes, but not in the traditional sense. The classes have already started, so you will be coming to my office for one hour, three days a week; and we're going to sort through your issues, as well as what you need to know to be confirmed." He stood up and started for the door.

"We'll start tomorrow if that works for you," he continued without missing a beat. All I could do was nod. "Then I'll see you tomorrow." With that, we shook hands, and I thanked him for seeing me. I made my appointment for the next day and left the office somewhat bewildered.

I walked the street engrossed in thought. I needed time to think about what had just happened to me. It seemed so crazy, but I felt like I had just sold my soul, what was left of it, for spiritual help. He had seemed genuinely interested in helping me, but maybe it was just some convert quota he had to fill. It shouldn't make any difference what religion I was, I thought. And I decided that it didn't really matter at that point what his motivation was. If he was after my soul, he could have it. It wasn't going to be of any use to anyone for a while, I was sure.

Looking back, I can clearly see that I desperately needed a process to jump start my life. Father Verderame's was readily available and as good as any, I reasoned. I went to a Catholic priest for help, and he had Catholicism to offer—what did I expect, Buddhism?

As I entered the courtyard, I noticed that Mother was home, and I ran up the stairs to tell her about my odd meeting. The minute I entered the house, though, I felt it: That same sixth sense I had used to detect trouble when I was a child. The Wolf was sensing something wrong. I took a deep breath and began to assess the situation.

"Hi, Mom," I said in a controlled, fake-happy voice.

She was standing in the kitchen eating a sandwich. As I approached, I noticed that she had made an extra one for me.

"I waited for a while but finally decided to go ahead and eat. I didn't know when you were coming home," she said, revealing nothing, though the air was heavy with significance.

"Thanks, I'm starving." I took the plate and went into the dining room. Something was definitely up, but I couldn't tell what it was.

"Morris Newberger called today to see how you were doing. I told him you were getting along fine," she said as she joined me in the dining room. Morris Newberger was the owner of the *Trashman*, and just the mention of his name made me uncomfortable.

"That's nice of him. What else did he have to say?"

The sandwich was going down without taste, and I recognized the sign: That meant that it could come back up without taste, too. It had been weeks since I'd done that.

"He said he was mailing you a check for the wages you earned on *Trashman*, plus a little extra to cover any out-of-pocket expenses. He also covered your hospital bills, since you don't have any insurance." She stopped, but I could tell there was more.

"Debbie, there are going to be some inquiries by Mr. Newberger's insurance company, as well as by the Coast Guard, and it looks like you'll have to make several statements. He really didn't know too much today, but said he would get back to us when he did know something."

"So, just what does all of that mean?" I asked, shoving potato chips into my mouth one after another. I hadn't thought about the Coast Guard in days, but the deep anger I felt was still fresh. I could feel the tension building in my chest. It was getting hard to breath.

"I don't know, but I guess we'll find out soon," she said, and, for a moment, the tension seemed to ease.

"Did Dr. Wiley call yet with the names of those shrinks?" I hoped I could just slide the question in unnoticed. But then I felt the tension thicken again.

"Actually, he did call. I told him that I really thought you had things under control and that it wouldn't be necessary right now. I said if we needed the names later, I'd get them from him then." With that, she picked up her plate and took it to the kitchen.

I wanted to scream. What business did she have telling him or anyone how I was doing? She didn't know. She never even asked how I was feeling. I didn't have anything under control—my whole life was out of control. It had been three weeks since the rescue, and it was all I could do to get to Saint Louis Cathedral and back.

"Mom, would you come in here for a minute and sit down? Please, I really need to talk to you." I felt the hair on my neck stand up. It was The Wolf: "Bad timing," said the voice in my head. "Don't do it now. She's not ready, and you'll only have one shot with her." But the moment's passion and the pain in my chest—the urgency of my need for help—pushed the warning aside.

She came back into the dining room and stood by the table nonchalantly.

"Sit down, please," I begged.

"I'm fine standing."

"Mom, I have real problems right now, and I need help. Please call Wiley back and get those numbers." I hated the fact that I had no money for doctors and was completely dependent on my mother at that moment. With all the money my family had, it seemed insane.

"You went to see the priest today. How did that go?"

"Mom, you're not hearing me. What I'm telling you is that I need some professional help. I feel like I'm losing my mind."

"Debbie, don't be so dramatic. You are not going to lose your mind. You heard Wiley yesterday. These things take time. It's only been a few weeks."

"Mom," I said looking up at her, "it's not just the sinking." A queasy, cold sweat surfaced on my skin. "I'm still bulimic, and we're not talking about several weeks, we're talking about eleven years, and it's killing me. I can't begin to deal with the sinking until I get this bulimia under control. You've been there. You've gotten treatment for your alcoholism, and look how great you're doing. I just want the same opportunity. I'm begging you—please help me." I watched for some emotion in her eyes, but she wouldn't look at me. She just gazed out the window. After an eternity of silence, she turned toward me.

"Debbie, you're twenty-four years old—an adult. I'm sorry about the sinking and I'm sorry about your eating disorder, but you don't have any health insurance, and I certainly can't afford to put you through treatment. Do you have any idea how much that would cost? You're just lucky that Morris Newberger picked up the tab for your hospital stay, or what would you have done?" She took a breath. "Speaking of which, you need to start thinking about what you're going to do with yourself after you've had a little more time to get over this ordeal."

It was just beginning to dawn on me how very strange our conversation was. My mother was rich. My family was rich. And yes, she was right, I had no health insurance. But I had never had health insurance, not even as a child. I wonder why. In fact, Mother didn't pay my college tuition or my brother

Lee's. When I was little, Daddy Jim paid for everything. I don't think my mother even paid when she sent me off to boarding school—who knows who paid for that.

And as I watched her reach over to pick up my plate and take it into the kitchen, I realized that I couldn't even remember receiving a Christmas or birthday card, much less a gift, from her in years. I got up and walked in after her. I decided to try one more approach.

"What do you think would have happened to you if you hadn't gotten treatment for your drinking?" I stared straight at her, waiting for her to look me in the eye. But she just kept rinsing the dish.

"My alcoholism has absolutely nothing to do with you or your present situation. At your age you need to take responsibility for yourself," she said without so much as a glance.

"But what about when you came to Morehead City and then brought me back here to recuperate? And then, the other night you said, 'That's what mothers are for.' Mom, if you don't help me, I could die. Remember Karen Carpenter? This is exactly what she died of." I was in tears, pleading.

"Debbie, I don't want to hear any more. My shrink warned me about bringing you back here, but I did it anyway. If you continue to bring this up, I'll have to ask you to leave." With that, she walked into her room and shut the door. And I rushed to the bathroom and threw up.

five

No More Victims

After my mother's ultimatum—"If you continue to bring this up, I'll have to ask you to leave"—I knew I had a real dilemma. On the one hand, I was in a position where I couldn't help but bring it up: Bulimia was ruling and ruining my life. On the other hand, I had nowhere to go, no money to get there, and nothing to do once I arrived. Plus I was reeling with the effort of trying to come to grips with who I was in the aftermath of the sinking.

Exhausted in mind and body, I threw myself completely into my spirituality. I spent hours and hours and hours every day in Saint Louis Cathedral.

I'd sit there, staring at the murals, trying to imagine how anyone could have painted those scenes while hanging upside-down on a scaffold. I kept coming back to one mural in particular. It showed an image of God as a bearded old man and the Holy Ghost as a dove surrounded by angels. Why did so many people think of God as an old white man wearing a flowing robe? It didn't match how I thought of God, whom I see as the universal energy that flows through all things. Even so, I found it to be a beautiful and comforting painting. It somehow made me feel peaceful. The gentle expression on God's face beckoned. The dove was so pure and white and perfectly rendered that it made me want to reach out and touch its soft feathers.

I sighed deeply. The God I knew was neither young nor old, neither human nor dove. He was just always there. He was my one and only loyal family, my protector, and my great teacher—although of late, I hadn't been really excited about the lessons I was having to learn.

God had spoken to me out on that raft. And now I was saying, "Okay, I'm here. Talk to me again. What's next?"

While I was cast away at sea, I had been so intensely focused on getting back to my mother that I hadn't allowed myself to think: What if she rejects me? Where do I go then?

I didn't know, and God wasn't saying. I hadn't made a Plan B. And now my mother had essentially rejected me yet again, saying in effect, "I really don't care if you die. Besides, it would cost too much to save your life." Maybe she really didn't care whether I lived or died; maybe she just didn't understand. Maybe I didn't understand her either.

She was right about something, though. I was twenty-four years old and should be able to take care of myself. Hell, I'd been taking care of myself all my life, anyway. What was so different now? It was time to make a Plan B.

After hours in that cathedral, my face aching from crying, my emotions drained, I finally sat up and gave myself a good talking to: I needed a new plan. I still had Father Verderame, whose spiritual support I so desperately needed. If that meant I had to become a Catholic, so be it. I held no particular preference for the Catholic Church over any other religion, but I had a good feeling about it from my childhood, and I needed a structure, a set of rules, a guide for knowing that somewhere, someone knew what was right and what was wrong. I desperately wanted to make some right choices in my life, and this structure would make some of them easy, because there were rules.

I looked up at the ceiling again to see the image of God in human form. The human body is such a magical machine to have survived all these thousands of years by simply continuing to adapt to its changing environment. Did adopting Catholicism and its teachings mean I had to give up my objective understanding of how we got here? I would have to remember to ask Father Verderame before this whole confirmation thing went any farther.

And while I was pondering this science/spirit split, how to balance what I knew with what I believed, I started thinking about survival. If survival is such a strong, innate drive, why would a human body sometimes choose to be self-destructive? Was the problem physical or mental, or both? If purely physical, chances are that the body's own immune system would fight to survive by making the necessary physiological adjustments or repairs. If the problem is mental, then it must be indicative of a sick spirit. But how could the body heal its own sick spirit? Was there any healing device, like the immune system, built in for the spirit? I couldn't imagine that God had created the human body and made the spirit dependent on economics and shrinks to heal it. Man had survived too long on this earth without them. If the human body could heal itself physically, surely it could heal itself mentally and emotionally, too.

This was it. Plan B. I had to find out how to heal my sick spirit.

I'd been in New Orleans about a month when I finished my tutoring with Father Verderame and became a Catholic. No sooner had I done so, then I decided in my bull-headed way that the thing to do now was to get right back on the horse, as the saying goes—to get back on the ocean immediately. Surely that would cure me.

I headed down to Florida for the fall Southern Ocean Racing Circuit. I signed on as cook for the sister ship that was to follow and assist one of the racing boats. Far from healing me, though, this promptly turned into the worst possible nightmare. A huge storm came up during one of the races, and several boats sank. A number of people were injured and killed. The whole dreadful experience made me that much more fragile and fearful.

Back on land in Florida, I spent almost all my time, every day, sitting or kneeling in a church, praying and praying. It was my only solace. I was staying in the house where the boat crew was living, just trying to keep my nervous system from frying itself, when Brad showed up. Seeing him was such a shock. I'd just come in out of a nasty ocean storm that had killed several people, and here came Brad, a ghost off the *Trashman*. Making matters worse, he was carrying a copy of *Sail* magazine with a big picture of Mark Adams on the front cover. He held it up and said, "Look. I told you he's the devil, and he's come back to haunt us."

I told him to get out. It was just too eerie. It even freaked out the other crew members in the house, who knew about the wreck of the *Trashman*. They were actively engaged in sailing and didn't want to see what could happen to them—what had happened to some of their fellow sailors in their most recent race.

Brad said, "You promised we'd always be together, and we're not."

"I'm trying to move on from this," I told him.

I knew what he wanted: He was trying to work through the same internal chaos as I was. But I couldn't help him. I had decided that if I didn't think about it or talk about it, it would just go away and I could pretend it had never happened. I had gone through my Catholic training to put up a buffer between the me I was now and the horrific thing I had gone through. Now I had my little rule book, and I was managing to abstain from bingeing and purging by telling myself that my body was God's gift to me and that I mustn't desecrate it. I now had the concept of sin to motivate me.

I was white-knuckling it through not only my addiction but my whole life as well. I was holding it together so tightly that I simply couldn't admit Brad into my life at that point—I was acting like my own mother: My own story was so noisy that I couldn't hear his story. He was too much of a reminder of what I'd been through. So I sent him away and went deep into my own denial.

⁂

After the Florida mess, I went back to New Orleans and found myself an apartment. I decided to get a job and take care of myself. It had always helped before. Pretty soon after, I met a wealthy guy and started dating him. He decided that it was unseemly for me to work as a waitress, and so he moved me into his house and told me I could take care of his boat to earn money.

So for a time, I rode my bicycle an hour and a half from his house to the dock and worked on his boat every day. The ride was therapeutic, but I could see that this was going to be a dead-end arrangement. I soon realized that this man was like one of those characters from my childhood, those men who spend rather than solve, buy rather than build. I couldn't grow or heal in this environment.

Brad's sister, Sarah Cavanagh, had once told me about a yacht design school she'd been to, the Landing School of Yacht Design in Kennebunkport, Maine. I decided to apply there. My rich guy had paid me well to take care of his boat, so I now had the money. When I was accepted, I said goodbye to him and drove to Maine.

I found a house and joined up with the hippie types who were attending the School of Yacht Design, and we drank and partied and designed yachts. Around that time, PBS asked me to participate in the filming of an episode of the educational series *The Voyage of the Mimi*. I really don't know how they even found me: I was a pro at hiding, and who in the world would have ever looked in Maine? Anyway, my episode was about shipwrecks. I had become the Shipwreck Lady.

In January, I went to a yacht design seminar in New York City and met John Kiley from Boston, who worked for a local yacht design firm—even though he really didn't have to work at all, because of several family trusts. With John too, something in our emotional systems recognized each other, drew us together, and that should have been warning enough for me: The warm and pleasant flow you're feeling is actually a rip tide. Eventually, I'd work out this rule for myself: Don't date anyone you're attracted to. But that was years away, and I still had many painful lessons to learn.

We had lunch, and he called me once I'd gone back to Maine, and he came to visit me there. Then I started visiting him in Boston, and he'd visit me in Maine, and we went on like that for a time. Then one day, I found out that I wasn't his only girlfriend; he was dating someone else as well.

A week later, a friend of mine accidentally ran over my dog, Grizzly. He not only killed him before my eyes as I watched out the window but then denied having done it.

Those two events, those two seeming betrayals, sent me into a severe depression and renewed my panic attacks. In retrospect, it probably could have been any adversity that would have set me off at that point: That's how precarious my balance was. I locked myself in my house and cried all day long. For days on end, I cried. I couldn't seem to stop.

Then I began eating and throwing up again, bingeing and purging. I thought I had put the bulimia behind me, vowing never to disrespect my body again, and now I felt completely out of control. In desperation, I called my mother, and she said she couldn't be bothered—she had her own problems. At the end of my rope, I called my real father back in Texas, and he sent me a ticket, and I went home.

I spent three weeks there, putting myself back together in the warmth and reality of my father's home, where people worked and cared for each other as a matter of course. I returned to normal eating habits and got some rest, praying constantly for guidance.

I knew I was still desperately trying to put the *Trashman* behind me. But what I didn't know was that in order to do that, I couldn't just forget it—I had to *understand* it. It had to have some meaning.

I had no idea how to give it meaning. I was still stuck on blame and denial. In that frame of mind, I hit on the idea of suing the Coast Guard. I reasoned that the key to understanding the whole *Trashman* episode was to figure out why the Coast Guard had abandoned us. Made perfect sense to me, because I didn't understand that the real answers to the *Trashman* lay within myself, deep in my own heart. I also had no idea what a miserable detour that legal action would become.

But it gave me something to do to busy myself. I can see now that I was grasping at anything—Catholicism, racing, yacht design, lawsuits—to take my mind off the central challenge of my life: To deal with what I'd been through.

I was on the run again, this time back to Maine to find a maritime lawyer who could handle the case.

In the spring of 1983 I reinstalled myself in Maine, dabbling in school, finding lawyers, commuting back and forth to Boston to date John Kiley. He was still dating two women, so I reasoned that I should be dating two men. I began dating a man named Stewart, who lived in Marblehead. Then John asked me to marry him. I accepted. I can't imagine what I was thinking.

The answer is: I wasn't. You don't need to think to make mistakes, you need to think to avoid them. I'm not saying John was a bad guy—he wasn't. Everyone has their problems, and sometimes they even mix, but mixing mine with his wasn't going to make either of us any better.

I kind of forgot to let Stewart know about the engagement; that too would come back to bite me.

The Newport-to-Bermuda race was coming up, and John had entered it, so I decided I should be there, too. John didn't need any crew. In fact, Brad was on his crew. But an old friend from the Whitbread did need someone, so I agreed to race on his boat.

I was steering the boat in the middle of the Gulf Stream in a nasty storm with waves breaking over me. I was facing my fear of the sea once more. And the sea once again had a lesson for me. Waves generally come in groups of three, and I had just endured the lashing of a big set, a real pounding, as I stood at the wheel, holding the boat on course. Relieved that they were over for the moment, I straightened up from a crouch, and unconsciously, I locked my left knee. When a fourth rogue wave came slamming down on me from behind, it hit so hard that it crushed my tibial plateau, crippling me.

There in the middle of the ocean, with no medical supplies, the crew taped my leg with a batten and sail tape. Since everyone else was seriously seasick, though, I had to keep on sailing anyway. I was scared to death, the weather was bad, I had a broken knee, and I didn't have a choice: It was mind over matter. I toughed it out.

When the race was over, I was taken to the hospital in Bermuda, where the doctors discovered that my injuries were so severe I was going to have to be flown to the mainland to undergo complicated surgery. The storm had not yet abated, and there was no way for me to get off the island yet. So I was waiting in the hospital room when Stewart arrived with an armload of roses. I had just opened my mouth to try to explain—when John Kiley walked in right behind him. After the embarrassing ordeal of having to listen to John and me explain that we were engaged, Stewart went away with his roses.

The doctors did the only thing they could for me until the weather cleared: They put a cast on my leg and gave me painkillers. John and I did not perhaps help the treatment by getting liquored up and renting a Moped. We went riding around the island in the rain for the next couple of days, high on painkillers and booze. My hip-length cast never even had a chance to dry.

Back in the U.S., I was hospitalized for seventeen days for major reconstructive surgery. I was essentially crippled until I could heal and rehabilitate my leg. Engaged to John Kiley, I was not yet married, so once again, in all-too-familiar pattern, I had nowhere to go.

I decided that the only thing to do was to go back to Texas, where my father's family could nurse me back to health. But John refused to allow it. I told him I couldn't continue to stay at his apartment if we weren't married—that was a Catholic rule.

John was Catholic, too. So that very day, he called a justice of the peace to marry us on the spot. A man named Ernest Guarantee—no kidding—showed up on D-Day, 1984, and married us in a civil ceremony with my leg propped up in a hip cast. Then John moved me to Cape Cod, where I spent the summer with his father and an old housekeeper, who took care of me.

It took my leg well into the fall to heal, and we planned a real wedding for November. Because we were both Catholics, we had to get our civil marriage annulled before we could get married officially in the Church. And sometime between then and our real wedding, I got pregnant. John and I were married for the second time on November 4, 1984. My first child, Marka, was born July 17, 1985. You can do the math.

John and I had moved into a house in Marshfield, Massachusetts, and were living the married life. On the surface at least. In reality, I was still white-knuckle flying, holding it together way too tight. I was adrift at sea in another kind of raft: My marriage.

By that time, the lawsuit, which had been grinding through the legal system for almost two years, had become so contentious, with accusations and threats flying back and forth, that the stress finally broke through my defenses. One morning when I was eight months pregnant with Marka, I was standing in the shower and simply began sobbing uncontrollably. Once again, I was having a nervous collapse.

Not knowing who to run to, I went to see my obstetrician, who took one look at me and said, "You're not just killing yourself, Debbie. You're killing this baby. You need to end this." So we settled the lawsuit right then and there. After all that, I still had no answers. Crucial communication records had mysteriously disappeared. The whole exercise had been futile, a grand diversion with no conclusion.

But at least it was behind me, and I settled down to take care of my new daughter. My life had been moving so fast that I thought certainly it would have to calm down now. But when Marka was three months old, I got pregnant again. I'd been told that you couldn't get pregnant while nursing. Well, apparently you could.

My son Quatro, short for John Coleman Kiley IV, was born July 23, 1986, and once again, the Kileys attempted to settle down to a normal life.

We were quite a pair, John and I. Anyone looking in from the outside could have predicted that our marriage would never work. There was plenty of money in John's family trusts, but the way it was doled out, it was enough for a single man to live in the style to which his family had allowed him to become accustomed, but it was not enough for a family to live that way. John's mother, for example, had given us a membership to the fanciest country club in the Boston suburb of Brookline, but we couldn't afford the dues. We were both from wealthy families, yet at times our electricity was shut off, because the bill hadn't been paid. John spent most of his time sailing and designing boats, while I stayed home with the kids and worried.

This all came to a head when the kids were one and two years old, and I contracted spinal meningitis. Once again, chronic stress and its impairment of my immune system put me in the hospital, followed by mandatory bed rest in a dark room for several months after. There was genuine concern that I might not make it. But I did.

When I began to recover, things were no better between John and me. He wasn't working, and there simply wasn't enough money to keep us afloat. In addition, I was miserable in Boston society. I was an outdoorsy ranch girl from Texas, and I just didn't fit in. I went back to Fort Worth in what might be called a trial separation and found a place to live. I stayed six months. John came down to visit around Easter. I really didn't know what to do. It was not in my nature to be a quitter, and divorce to my mind was a form of giving up.

I awoke in bed with my husband on Easter morning. He was still asleep when I opened my eyes and sat up. And there at the foot of my bed was Jesus. I know it sounds crazy—and maybe it is—but He was standing right there at the foot of my bed. The Jesus who appeared to me looked like the painting on the ceiling of Saint Louis Cathedral.

I looked at Him and heard Him say, "Go back. You have to go back and try, or you'll never forgive yourself. And I'll let you know when your time is up." Well, I thought, if Jesus bothers to appear to you and tell you to do something, you'd better do it. So I went back to Boston, bent on saving our three-year-old marriage.

I found a marriage counselor and went to the sessions religiously. John came a few times but didn't seem that interested. For six years we were in and out of counseling. Then he stopped showing up at all. Finally, one day, the counselor asked me sincerely, "Debbie, what are you doing here?"

I said, "I'm trying to fix my marriage."

"You just said two key words," she told me. "'I' and 'fix.' I've never told anybody this before," she continued, "but you need to move on."

About that time, I went back to visit Texas and saw my Uncle Jim Calhoun, who was not really an uncle but a dear family friend. Uncle Jim looked at me and said, "Debbie, I've never seen someone try so hard. It's time to move on."

But I still wasn't ready to admit defeat. I started seeing psychiatrists, thinking that if I couldn't fix my marriage, maybe I could fix myself. But each one I saw tried to tell me my problems were all based on sexual dysfunctions. They were all confirmed Freudians, and I found their explanations ridiculous.

At last, I found a therapist named Anamika who gave me the idea of going back through my memories to try to put them to rest. It was around that time, in 1992, that I began thinking about writing a book about the sinking of the *Trashman*. And as our financial situation at home deteriorated to the point that we were literally running on fumes, I decided that somebody had to make some money or we'd lose our home. I made up my mind to write a book—and sell it. It was something I felt I could do. It was something I felt I needed to do: It had been ten years since the sinking. I had to get the story out of me. And I had to support myself and my children without depending on anyone else.

Everybody thinks marrying money, big money, must be great. I didn't know John had any money before we were married. And I sure wasn't happy about the life that went with all that money. Particularly since it was a moneyed lifestyle rather than any real money that we had. We started living in this crazy, hedonistic world where people went to "the Cape" every summer, and slept with each other's wives or husbands, drinking themselves into a stupor every night, mothers screwing the camp counselors—it was my crazy childhood all over again. To be fair, not everyone was like that; many were quite nice and helped keep me from going over the edge. But in general, it was a crazy life—made particularly insane by not having the wherewithal to keep it up. I just had to get away from it.

I bought one of the early laptop computers, a Toshiba Satellite, and began writing furiously, pouring out my story, purging myself of the venom I'd been bingeing on for so long. I discovered that I loved writing. Suddenly, I wasn't holding on for dear life anymore. I was letting go.

I'd stay up long into the night, pouring my heart out. And if I went to bed early, I'd wake in the middle of the night and start writing again. It was as if I were possessed. But it was a therapeutic possession. I had found the meaning I'd been looking for. It had been right under my nose all along: Just tell what happened. Tell it truthfully and passionately, without shame or blame.

The strange and wonderful thing was that the book sold almost immediately. When it was published, under the title *Albatross: The True Story of a Woman's Survival at Sea*, I went on

Larry King Live, *Inside Edition*, and lots of other shows. I was in demand on the speaking circuit, making good money to talk about my experiences before audiences large and small. It was so liberating to tell my story and to have people listen and accept it and even embrace it. I was freeing myself from long years of silence. I'd found purpose in my life.

And that's when the gloves really came off between me and John. Because my success drove him absolutely nuts.

When we went to Cape Cod that summer, all anyone wanted to talk to us about was my book. I knew John was building up to some sort of crisis, because of all the attention I was getting and the money I was making. Our egos were eating away at each other. I could see the dark clouds gathering on the horizon of our already stormy marriage.

And then I was invited onto Oprah's show. That is the holy grail for authors and an extremely long shot. There's so much demand to get on that show, and here I'd done it. I had the same feeling I had when I was invited to sail the Whitbread Around the World Race. I was so excited I went out and bought a really expensive bottle of wine, and I was at home cooking this fabulous pasta dinner, when John came in. I wanted to share my joy with him, so I said, "Guess what."

I saw his face darken, and he said, "What? You fucking got Oprah?"

I knew he hadn't been told. He'd just been waiting, fearing the moment of my ultimate success, dreading it, hating it. At that moment, he was like a cornered animal. And it frightened me. So I tried to salvage the moment and said, "How did you know?" still trying to sound cheerful.

But he stormed out, got his in car, and backed out of the driveway, tires screaming. He drove so fast that he nearly ran over my dog, who went scurrying away. (Why do men always want to kill my dogs?)

The next thing I knew, my best friend was calling on the phone. She told me that John had come over there, and that he was really angry and that it might be a good idea for me to take the kids and go to the Cape for a night or two. And for a moment, I thought of doing it: Yes, run. That's what Mother and I had always done when I was a child. We ran and ran from the crazy, violent men. It's what I'd always done growing up. It's what I did when I raced across the country to catch the last voyage of the *Trashman*. I'd run to New Orleans, run to Florida, run to Maine for yachting school, run back to Texas to recover…

But wait a minute: I had children now. And I'd proven myself by writing *Albatross*. I was earning my own money. I was going on *Oprah*, and the freight train that was my life had to stop right here. I just wasn't going to run anymore. Most especially not from a man throwing a temper tantrum.

I told her, "No, I'm not going to do that. I'm going to lock myself in, and you need to tell him right now: Do not come back here." The next day, I called my lawyer and filed for divorce. And in 1996, after a couple of ugly years of legal and psychiatric wrangling, I found myself before a judge. Several days later, it was over.

I grew up among the biggest liars in the world. I grew up listening to them lie all the time. I watched them continually break faith and break promises. And I grew up bound and determined not to lie. I always try to keep my word. I wanted to leave the Whitbread race so desperately on that last leg I could hardly stand it. But I'd given my word and made a commitment. And when I got my divorce, it was the hardest thing I'd ever done. Besides, I was Catholic: I thought marriage was for life. And I hated being a quitter. But it was my only choice. John wasn't a bad guy. It was just that our marriage had become a lie.

I stuck with it for eight years after our first separation, because I had practiced hiding my feelings for so long and had practiced letting crazy people be as crazy as they liked and not feeling that I had the power to do something about it. And I knew from all that practice that I'd probably struggle through and be fine. I was conditioned to that crazy atmosphere and had learned a bad lesson: That I can survive it.

But now I'd learned another lesson, too: Sometimes the best survival strategy is to avoid catastrophe in the first place. That means getting off the sinking ship *before* it goes down.

Then and there I made a decision that would become my new motto in life: *No more victims.*

When it was over, I took the children and moved to Fort Worth, bought a house, and went back to college, where I finished my degree. I graduated summa cum laude with a 3.88 average. My degree was in interdisciplinary studies, and I thought I might go into advertising. But I had always been a fanatic about fitness, and I didn't find the corporate world a very comfortable fit, so I became a master fitness specialist, certified by the Cooper Clinic, and began working at a local gym as a personal trainer.

Trashman was over. Marriage was over. Running was over. I'd told my story. I'd found my home at last. The nightmare was over.

Well, for the most part.

six

The Imperfect Storm

One morning in the spring of 2000, I found myself on the treadmill, thinking: Now what? I had really come a long way. With all I'd been through, I ought to be a hundred years old by now. But I was in great physical and mental condition, my kids were healthy, well-adapted honor students at a good private school. God had answered my desperate childhood prayers: I was actually happy. What more could a person want?

Every survival journey is preparation for the next, and there was a nagging feeling that something was missing. I had decided after four years of dating that it definitely wasn't a man. And I had spent countless days searching the Internet and emailing resumes looking for that perfect job, while my friends harped at me to write another book. *Albatross* had been made into a movie—a very bad movie—and the whole Hollywood experience had soured me on writing. Hollywood is famous for that, but as with everything, I'd had to learn that first hand to believe it.

When nothing much is happening in your life—particularly when you've had such a tumultuous life as I've had, or when you've just gone through some really peak experience that took all your energies—it's tough to know if that lull means passive inactivity or deep internal processing. In other words, are we just drifting, or are we learning and preparing for the next big challenge to come?

That evening, my friend Julie showed up with a copy of Marianne Williamson's *Illuminata: A Return to Prayer*. When I opened the cover, there was a note from her that read, "A beautiful book of asking and rejoicing for a beautiful soul who deserves completeness. Love always, Julie."

I was deeply touched—and inspired. I desperately needed to find a new creative outlet for my life, one that would allow me to express and extend the blessings in my life to others. And now this sign had suddenly appeared: "A beautiful book of asking..."

If you want to work for someone, you have to ask for a job. So I asked God for a job; and Julie's gift, *Illuminata*, gave me the words in the form of a beautiful prayer.

Several weeks later, standing in my kitchen, engrossed in preparing my favorite lasagna recipe, I felt an energizing warmth envelop my body. I stopped and waited, wondering what it was. Then I was infused with an incredible sense of peace. I felt an overwhelming gratitude for the extra years of life I'd been given, for I had accomplished more in the eighteen years that had followed the sinking of the *Trashman* than I had even dreamed of in the first twenty-four years of my life. I was healthy and happy and had risen above bulimia and madness. I was no longer holding on white-knuckled for dear life. I was floating in a state of grace.

At peace and suffused in the glow of gratitude, I heard a little voice in my head say: "It's your job to keep the miracle alive, to share the lessons you've learned." It was suddenly all so clear. For years, I had been consciously and unconsciously studying the effects of diet, exercise, spirituality, prayer, visualization, and meditation as part of an ongoing process of dealing with my own demons. For the last several months, I had struggled to give a new creative meaning to my life.

And now my path began to reveal itself.

Around this time, the big-budget action movie *The Perfect Storm* came out. Based on the true story of a fishing boat caught in the middle of three storm fronts which then loses all of its crew after a valiant fight against the elements, it was uncomfortably close to home. But it was all the rage that summer, and I figured I could face my fear. So I went to see it with the man I was dating at the time.

I truly believed that after all those years, I could handle it. But as the storm raged on the screen, I could once again smell the stench of urine and Meg's rotting flesh. I could hear the screeching gull overhead as it dropped down to peck at Meg's face. I could feel the churning waves and the sharks lifting the boat to spill us into the sea. And I felt a primal sadness enter me. How could I still be so vulnerable? How was it possible that these memories could still be so invasive? Sitting in the theater seat, I felt my personality begin to divide and fragment. Salty tears pooled in the corners of my mouth, reminding me of my insatiable thirst while adrift at sea. My boyfriend kept asking me if I wanted to leave, but I stubbornly held on. I had to stay. I had to feel the emotions.

As the movie went on, though, my emotions changed from despair to anger. This movie didn't show what it was like to survive. It was a pale, plastic Hollywood version of reality, tarted up with big-name stars and trite dialogue. Who did these people think they were to mock authentic experience with such nonsense?

When the movie ended and I finally felt somewhat composed, we got up from our seats and started out of the theater. But before we even reached the door, we ran into one of my boyfriend's business associates. Oh God, I thought, not now. I couldn't face anyone at that moment. I bolted for the restroom without saying a word, tears streaming down my face. I fell through the door and looked around. It was empty. For a brief moment I felt safe. Then in the starkness of the tile room, blasted with fluorescent light, I caught a glimpse of my blotchy, tear-stained face. I was falling apart. The memories had been triggered and the demons unleashed. "Pull it together, Debbie, you're tougher than they are. Just pull it together." My words echoed off the tiles. But for the first time in years, I felt frightened. I knew I really wasn't tougher than the demons, because the demons were part of me.

On our way to the movie, my boyfriend had tried to warn me about tempting fate by stirring up old memories. But, as always, I had to test the waters. And now I knew. The pain was still there.

Standing there in the restroom, I realized I had opened Pandora's box. I had survived the sinking of the *Trashman*, and I had survived surviving, but had I really learned the lessons of a survivor?

That night we sat out in the hot, humid Texas dark and watched the stars. We talked about the incredible grip death can hold on life. Death is the only predictable and inevitable part of God's plan, yet it is what humans fear most. Science constantly searches for ways to eradicate death, but to no avail. Death remains the ultimate destination in life's journey, the place where all paths meet.

Starry Texas nights were made for philosophizing, and we were both self-proclaimed scholars of death. My boyfriend had lost his older sister to childbirth when he was in high school; and, just as I lived each day with the memories of the sinking, he, too, was a daily captive of past suffering. We thought how ironic it would be if in what we feared the most and worked the hardest to avoid—death—we ultimately would find the very thing we so passionately sought our whole lives—peace.

The movie had scared and shaken me, but I vowed that I would not go back to that place of terror again, not tonight, not ever. I would hold my vigil till dawn. Morning would bring a new beginning, and by then I would be well into survival mode—my lifeline of survival skills forged in pain, cast in flesh, and always available at a moment's notice.

I realized anew that the things that seemed so horrible in my life were what had created the survivor in me. Everyone has horrible things to contend with; as Antoine de Saint-Exupery said, even our misfortunes are part of our belongings. The only way to escape suffering is to die. To embrace life with all its joy and all its sorrow is the only way to live. The lesson, then, is to learn to turn all life's experiences into opportunities. And to let those experiences teach you your survival skills.

Gradually, my fear and my anger gave way to a completely different feeling. As dawn came up, turning the Texas sky a hazy pink, I thought: I'm there. I've washed up on shore at last.

Two weeks later, my publisher called to say they were reissuing *Albatross* (under the title *Untamed Seas*) and asking if I'd ever thought about writing another book, a book on how I had survived in the aftermath. I said yes, yes, I had.

I was nearly ready.

seven

A Sea of My Own

Although I no longer felt that I needed a man or had to have a husband or even a boyfriend, everybody in Fort Worth kept trying to fix me up with dates. The town was just full of matchmakers.

It's not like I'd been a hermit for all those years of being a single mom. I'd dated a guy—another John—who was thirteen years younger than I was. He was cute, and we had great fun, riding horses out on the range. But I knew it could never go anywhere: He was too young; we couldn't share enough experiences. We dated for two years, and then I got out.

Then I dated a man who had five children from two previous wives and was abusive, controlling, and a general nightmare. He was so wrong for me that I went and got engaged to him just for good measure. Fortunately, my family counselor, Mary Jane Hooper, made me see what a mistake I was on the verge of making, and I realized, "Oh, my God. It's all the men in my mother's life. It's my whole insane childhood!" So I quickly broke off the engagement, pleased and relieved that, this time, I hadn't even boarded what was sure to be a sinking ship.

I refused steadfastly to date guys from town. Fort Worth is just like Peyton Place: no secrets and no privacy; I didn't want to be served up for breakfast gossip. But one day in the spring of 2002, a woman came up to me in the gym and said, "I've watched you for a long time, and you've got to meet my brother-in-law. You'd be perfect for each other." I told her that I didn't date people in Fort Worth and saw the look of surprise on her face. "You don't?" she asked disappointedly.

My son Quatro was about to go off to boarding school, too, and I started to think about it: With my kids gone, it probably wouldn't matter who I dated. And the woman at the gym kept coming back, insisting I meet her brother-in-law. So I finally relented. She said he'd stop by some time.

One day, without any warning, this big guy came in, six-three, very fit and handsome in a rugged way, wearing khaki pants and a yellow polo shirt. I'd seen him pull up in his big BMW. He seemed just a bit cocky.

I had just been for a run and was all sweaty, wearing no makeup, and here comes this huge guy, who walked up and said, "Hi, I'm Greg Blackmon." And frankly, I could tell that he was more impressed with himself than I was. I was not interested. We chatted for a minute or two, and then he left.

And that would have been that, except that the sister-in-law kept coming back, saying, "Ya'll have gotta go out." So Greg and I tried, and our schedules didn't match, and it took a while for us to connect.

When we finally did, though, we ended up having a ball. He was so different from anyone I'd ever gone out with before, and a little voice of intuition told me that that was a good thing. Greg was kind, generous, and self-assured—no fragile ego, no raging child to contend with. I didn't have to be on my guard around him. He was a complete person, an equal, not someone who needed me to plug a leak in his sinking vessel, a hole in his soul.

He was also a self-made man who had come up from hard-working people, not from money. His family was stable and knew the value of things. His father had worked his way up from nothing, going to college on a football scholarship and starting a small upholstery and cleaning business. When Greg and his brothers took over, it was a thriving business that included carpet and duct cleaning, and it started them on the road to becoming the foremost disaster recovery business in the world. They have cleaned up after floods, fires, hurricanes, airline crashes, and they cleaned up after 9/11 and the World Trade Center disaster, too.

That year, Greg and I frequently rode our bikes around his neighborhood and the TCU campus. During our rides, we passed this beautiful house with a bluff view—and a "for sale" sign. Greg had been thinking about moving, so we set up an appointment to see the house. We loved it.

That night, we were cooking dinner at Greg's house, and he said, "Let's make an offer on that house."

"Look," I said. "I'm not moving into that house with you if we're not married. And I don't remember you ever asking me to marry you."

He got a surprised look on his face, and said, "I didn't?"

"No."

"Well, come here and sit down," Greg said.

"No way," I said. "I want a ring. And you're going to at least take me to a restaurant."

"Okay," he said. "Go pick out a ring tomorrow."

He didn't have to tell me twice. At the jewelry store the next day, I picked out three rings, small, medium, and large. When Greg saw them, he said, "You really like the big one, don't you?"

I said, "A ring is a ring is a ring, but yeah. I like the big one."

And Greg said, "Okay." That's the way Greg is: no games, no pretense. And he really does care what I want.

That night, he said, "Let's go to dinner."

"But the ring's not ready," I protested.

"That's okay, I've improvised."

I didn't know what he had in mind, but we went to Silver Fox Steak House, and, when the waiter came over, Greg turned to me and asked, "Okay, do I have to get you champagne or what?"

"That would be nice."

"I'll have a beer," he told the waiter, "and she'll have champagne." When our drinks came, he lifted his glass and said, "Okay, I don't want to mess this up: Will. You. Marry. Me?"

"Yes," I said.

Then he reached in his pocket and pulled out the ring: It was a notebook binder ring from Office Depot all wrapped in tape to make it fit. When he slipped it on my finger, I asked, "Is this in lieu of the other ring?"

"No," he said. "It'll just last a few days until you get the real thing." I still have the notebook binder ring.

When I was out on the Zodiac after the wreck of the *Trashman*, the entire world was the uniform gray of the sea. For all those days, moving relentlessly toward my own death, I watched that metallic gray world and longed for something green, something growing, that I could feast my eyes on. My hunger for color grew almost as intense as my thirst for water.

Now as I look out my window into my Zen garden, I see my dogs, Rosie and Parker (as in Richard Parker, the Bengal tiger in *Life of Pi* and, need I mention, a pound dog), and crazy Pearlene (the pound cat who thinks she's a dog), my pond with my Koi in it, and beyond that the enormous view that is a sea of green. And that, today, is my ocean. I wake up to it each morning and think back on my life and am filled with amazement and gratitude for this miracle that is my life. I even have Chelsea and Alex, the two more kids I always wanted—without the pain of childbirth. I marvel at how I got here from the Bermuda Triangle of Texas. I don't believe that Neil Armstrong setting foot on the moon for the first time marveled any more than I do today.

I walked out this morning, and there was this scent in the air, and as I breathed it in, I thought: Wow. I'm alive. I'll forever search for what the true meaning of my life has been, but I think I know now, and it's so simple it evaded me for decades: The meaning is to continue searching. The path never ends. But I think that simply telling it, passing on the lessons, is part of it. I wish everybody knew how good life is. For some, like me, it takes something catastrophic to wake you to this wonder. But there are other ways to get there, too.

In many ways, survival is not simply the act of surviving something that might kill you. It's the passion for life that keeps you living. It is the journey of discovering your own will to live. Along the way on this journey, you release your fear of death, set it aside, and let go in order to discover exactly how much you really do want to live. And having discovered that, having then lived fully, it is the unending immersion in that life, the transformation of fear into fully experiencing it all, embracing the pain and joy with equal openness, for we live in that space, and that truly is what life is: The endless journey between pain and joy and back again, on and on, until we greet death with a full heart for a life well lived.

Everyone can take lessons from life. This book merely represents a few of my own.

eight

Another Storm: My Mother and Katrina

As I watched the news Sunday morning, August 28, my intuition told me it was going to be bad. Greg and I were still in Washington, D.C., getting my son Quatro settled in his college dorm, when it became apparent that Hurricane Katrina would come ashore right on top of New Orleans—or at the least, very near the city. My jaw dropped as I watched the swirling orange mass with the intense crimson center, ugly, growing. It looked as if the Gulf had caught fire, and those intense rotating winds were capable of destroying everything in their path.

I hadn't spoken to my mother in a year. She still lived in New Orleans. And as I watched the TV radar image, the fierce red flower of Katrina surging across the Gulf looked like an enormous angry fist... It seemed like the wrath of an Old Testament God aimed straight at my mother.

No, that can't be, I thought. That's not even the God I believe in. I knew I shouldn't have thoughts like that. Even after all the years of entanglement with her—pleading, begging, fighting, cajoling—after decades of listening to her delusions and lies, of suffering her abuse and neglect and insanity—I didn't hate her. I certainly didn't wish her any harm. I can't say that I really like my mother, but in my heart I do love her.

As I watched the TV, I noticed something else: The storm was enormous. It was the size of Arkansas. I was hypnotized by its power, and reminded of another storm, one whose memory is always with me. My God, I thought, is she stubborn enough to stay and face the storm? What if it kills her? Despite everything, I didn't want to lose my mother. I had to know where she was.

I knew her number by heart, but when I dialed it, I only got a recording—"We're sorry, all circuits are busy. Please try your call again later."

A few hours later, Greg, Quatro, and I were having brunch when the subject of the hurricane came up again. Quatro pulled out his phone and began dialing a friend of his who was in his first year at Tulane University. He connected with him on the first try. So I immediately pulled out my phone and tried Mother again. When I heard the same recording, I felt it must be an omen. I should leave well enough alone, I told myself. But I just couldn't stop, and I dialed again.

Greg finally asked, "Who do you keep calling?"

I almost hated to answer. "Mother," I said.

He gave me a dumbfounded, questioning look and said, "Okaaaay."

But I could feel the trepidation in his voice. We both knew too well how decades of trying had failed to reconcile me and my mother. If my hurricane had failed to do it, why should her hurricane be any different? But that was another of my survival lessons: Never give up.

That evening Greg and I said goodbye to Quatro and headed back to Fort Worth. The airport was abuzz with news of the storm, and the radar images glowed on every television screen we passed. We struck up a conversation with a woman sitting across from us as we waited to board. She was a psychotherapist who specialized in eating disorders. Such coincidences no longer even took me by surprise. It was as if I was reliving all the most dramatic parts of my life in bits and pieces through Katrina—the bulimia, the sinking, the running, and of course the never-ending drama of my mother.

I reached over and took Greg's hand. Even as we sat there waiting for our plane, crews from his company, the foremost disaster cleanup outfit in the world, were headed down to staging areas close to the Gulf so they'd be poised and ready to move the moment the storm passed. If need be, they could swoop down on Mother's apartment and snatch her—kicking and screaming no doubt—from the jaws of disaster.

I excused myself and went to the restroom to call her again. Nothing.

Surely she would have enough sense to follow the mandatory evacuation order. I wondered if she was self-destructive enough to stay put just to spite everybody. Her ability to deny reality was breathtaking, but I hoped that if she saw on her television what I saw on mine, she'd get the message.

I tried one last time—again without success—as we boarded the plane. Before we took off, I used the Internet on my phone to check the weather. Katrina was even worse—larger, redder, angrier. And it was heading straight for New Orleans.

To me, the storm was much more than an abstract image on a screen. I had seen up close what the sea could do, had felt its blind fury as it smashed through wood and steel. I had known its frenzied determination as it tried to take me away from everything I had ever known and loved. I'd seen it kill my shipmates. I remembered well those black marble waves, towering above me, and could still feel the pile-driver mass which could split bone and callously deliver a body to the sharks.

As Greg and I headed for home, I thought of all those people down there on the Gulf. Most of them likely didn't know it yet, but they were about to have an experience just like mine after the *Trashman* sunk. Many of them were about to die—perhaps thousands. Many others were about to find out what they were made of. And they were all about to have their lives changed forever. Looking down on the world from thirty thousand feet up with the images of Katrina vivid in my mind, it was terrifying to know what I knew.

But where was Mother?

The minute we got home that night, I turned on the television and surfed the channels, as if I might see something different, perhaps stumble on some station where the storm had miraculously vanished and the world was calm again. I called and called Mother's home in vain. Of course, with the storm that close, the circuits were jammed. I wasn't surprised—just pissed. Was she doing this on purpose? Refusing to call anyone? Or was she just so forgetful, so out of touch, that it hadn't occurred to her to call? Or was she dead?

I was unable to sleep that night, waiting for morning to come. There was no question that the storm was going to make landfall at or very near New Orleans. Maybe then I'd get the call from some posh hotel, saying that she and Molly, the dog I'd given her, were safe. That's how mother liked to ride out hurricanes—in luxury.

By six o'clock Monday morning, I was stationed in front of the television with my cup of tea, watching Katrina grind slowly toward New Orleans. Her slow progress over the warm water of the Gulf had pushed her to a Force Five hurricane—the biggest of the big.

I had breakfast and decided to go to a yoga class. I just couldn't stand the waiting. As I drove to class, I realized how very angry I was at her, all the years, all the miles, all the tears and blood spilled. I hated it that she could still get inside me like this just by not calling. And as I stewed, the memories began to flood my mind.

I'm a little girl, and it's the middle of the night. A storm is raging. Howls and screams and slamming doors split the silence of the remote ranch where we live. Headlights flood the yard, and gravel flies, as the truck roars away into the night. One of my puppies is dead, and the other is hobbling around, crushed and bleeding, and I'm screaming, "Get the gun! Get the gun!" because I knew we'd have to put the poor little dog out of his misery. Then I was I quivering in bed, and Mother had the gun clutched in her hand, and I was weeping, terrified.

Soon highway patrol officers were at the door, and there were whispers and warnings and phone calls. I was a small child, but I knew that as bad as it had been already tonight, it was going to get worse. My mother's third husband—my abuser—had a gun and was on his way. We had to run. We piled a few belongings into the car and tore off into the night, down the long sleepless roads, past the moonlit diners and glowing gas stations and on up into the mountains, seeking out higher ground, leaving dead puppies in our wake.

Remembering all this as I drove to my friend Brooke's yoga studio, it suddenly occurred to me that Mother was just a little girl, too. Not just then, when she was only in her twenties, but always. She'd never grown up, never been allowed to by her parents. She was just a terrified little girl, running in the night from the demons—very real ones with very real guns—who pursued her.

Only recently had I tried to find out what her childhood had been like. It wasn't just her father who made her life hell—the drunken rages, the beatings, the nonstop psychological abuse, the unspeakable incest. It was her mother, too, a mean and stubborn woman, who would pile her daughter's plate so high with food that it would have taken a ranch hand all day to eat it. And then she'd make my mother sit and eat for hours in a contest of wills, while the other children played. My mother wept pitifully but was not allowed to leave until she'd eaten it all. Sometimes she'd try to slip a bite to one of the dogs under the table, and, if she was caught, she was taken to the back room and beaten until her screams filled the house.

The truly odd thing was that my grandmother herself had an eating disorder, long before anyone even had a name for it. All her life she was rail thin, because, obsessed with her figure, she only ate every other day. When she became pregnant with my mother, she stopped eating altogether in order to maintain her weight. She ate only lettuce for months on end, with the result that my mother was born premature at three pounds and spent the first weeks of her life in the hospital. She never had a chance to bond with her mother during those all-important early days. Not that her mother would have allowed it anyway. But it struck me for the first time: My grandmother, who refused to eat even while pregnant, force-fed her own little girl, my mother, who in turn had force-fed me. The eating disorders, like everything else, had been passed down through the generations.

Her parents had systematically cut the love out of that little girl before she even had a chance to know what it was like. She was the object of such constant and heartless abuse that, as a child, she was a mass of physical ticks. If my grandfather reached up to scratch his head, she'd flinch. By the time she was in first or second grade, she was practically mute, afraid to speak. She wasn't allowed to have friends. And she was never out of sight of her father, who watched her like a hawk. One of my mother's cousins told me of seeing her father slap my mother so hard when she was a little girl that she literally flew across the room. My mother's mother, in turn, was furiously jealous of their incestuous relationship, and made it her mission in life to torture my mother for revenge, because she was afraid to stand up to her own husband.

Thinking of all this, absorbing its reality for the first time, I felt a tremendous wave of sympathy for my mother. I wanted to hold her, enfold her, to take away all the decades of pain and confusion in one gigantic sweeping wave like the wave that was about to wipe New Orleans off the map. That poor little girl had never had a chance. I was born when she was seventeen, still a child herself. She may have even gotten herself pregnant to keep her father away from her. I'd never know.

Brooke's yoga studio always brought me a great sense of comfort, but comfort was in scarce supply today. As we stood with our hands folded in an attitude of prayer, Brooke asked us to remember those who were in the path of Katrina, and I was suddenly hit by this image of my mother as the Wicked Witch of the West in *The Wizard of Oz*, flying through the storm on her broom, and I laughed out loud. Humor in the face of disaster leads to salvation. Fly away, little girl, I thought. Fly away to safety.

An hour later, I was on the phone to my grandmother, who, at ninety-two, is very hard of hearing. But I finally got her to understand that there was a bad hurricane and that I was trying to find my mother—her daughter. I was stunned into silence when she told me that my mother had moved—without telling her or anyone else where she'd gone. I felt a tremendous wave of sadness for Mother: She was so alone in the world that she could move from one city to another and not even feel the need to call her mother or her children or her grandchildren. As I watched the storm slam into New Orleans, at least I knew she was somewhere else, wherever that might be. I went to bed that night convinced that, no matter where she was, my mother was probably just fine.

When I turned on the news the next morning, however, I could scarcely believe what I was seeing. Water was filling the city. I saw boats on top of houses, oil rigs slammed into highway overpasses, people walking through waist-deep water, others shooting at police. I ran upstairs to wake Greg, but he was already watching.

I called my mother's brother, Ross, at his office. Ross was out of town, but I managed to find out from his secretary that Mother was alright, even though she wouldn't tell me where she was. Ross probably wouldn't have told me either.

I sat watching the news, feeling stupid for having wasted all that time and energy on her: Duped again. With tears in my eyes, I glanced up at the television in my kitchen. I had never seen a hurricane dole out this much destruction.

Then I saw an image I'll never forget: A Coast Guard helicopter swooped in and hovered over the roof of a submerged house where a group of survivors had broken through the attic roof and were waving frantically. I watched as a rescuer was lowered on a cable and joined those survivors on the roof. Then he unhooked himself and sent the cable back up to the helicopter. A man at the helicopter's open door attached a litter to the cable and lowered it to the roof. One by one, the team of rescuers raised the survivors to the helicopter until they'd all been saved.

As I continued to watch the Coast Guard lift victims from the sunken houses, I was struck with awe. I couldn't help but feel an overwhelming respect and gratitude for what they were doing. But more than anything, I felt a true sense of forgiveness: I saw the Coast Guard in a new light. Whatever had happened to me in the Atlantic Ocean, I could not deny the reality of what I was seeing now. If my mother had been on one of those roofs—if I'd been—they would have saved her—and me too.

And I saw, too, that my mother had been stranded without rescue for much longer than I had been. She'd been held prisoner on that remote ranch, tortured by her demon-ridden mother and father. In answer, my mother had done the only thing she knew how to do: Escape and keep on escaping. Even now, moving from New Orleans without telling anyone: I had to respect that as an act of survival, going with her gut, listening to her intuition. She'd been through wars I could only imagine.

I'd been going about this all wrong. I couldn't earn my mother's acceptance, or win that mythical relationship I'd always wanted. I could only master the situation by mastering myself: I could forgive her. And I could only reconcile myself with the Coast Guard by forgiving them, too.

During the next three days, as I watched the mayhem unfold, I gradually reaffirmed and confirmed my feelings of forgiveness. My mother had struggled heroically as a child against forces impossibly larger than herself. Every day was a fresh hurricane when she was a child. I wished the Coast Guard could have hovered over that ranch and lowered a basket to pull her out.

I saw now that not even her own mother had tried to save her. There had been no midnight escapes from her insane father. At least *my* mother had taken my hand, put me in the car, and driven me to Vail. She had tried to save me. In her own way, she was struggling to break the cycle. I realized that she had done the best she could with what she had at the time. And that was all any of us could do. That's survival: Take a breath and do the best you can with what you've got.

Oh, Mother: I wish I could have been there for you.

It was Friday just before noon, five days after Katrina made landfall, when Mother called at last. I was so glad to hear her voice. It seemed like a new relationship, but I realized it was just a new me, my new attitude. I couldn't change the world. I could only change my response to it.

Mother and I talked several times that day, and I learned that she hadn't given up her apartment in New Orleans. She'd just gone to Reno for the summer. All of her belongings were still back on Saint Joseph Street. I assured her that when things settled down, Greg's guys would get in there and salvage whatever was left. She thanked me and then told me what I'd just come to realize in the past few days, as if she'd been reading my mind. She said that she had done the best she could and that for whatever it was worth, my brother and I had both turned out great. And before we hung up, she said something to me that I had wanted to hear my entire lifetime.

She said that she was proud of me.

nine
Surfacing

One thing I've finally figured out about life: If we don't learn our lesson the first time, we will be faced with it again and again and again.

I had been raised in a very dangerous world and had learned at an early age that I had to do things for myself all the time. I learned to control my environment—by running away and hiding, for example. And when Grandmother Queenie would hold me in her arms while I cried and tell me that everything was going to be alright, I learned something else: This, too, will pass.

For years I ran wild, but running was not my intention. My intention was to be free of a painful childhood and to be at peace with who I was—whoever *that* was. I wanted my own story and someone who would listen to it and accept it. Yet I had learned at a very early age that humans were not to be trusted. Five divorces equaled five dysfunctional fathers and one very dysfunctional mother. Add to that moving from place to place, too much booze, too much fighting, shots fired in anger, screaming tires, dead pets, police in the night, clammy flesh, and the cold blue-black barrel of a .357 pressed against virgin skin. An accumulation of circumstances had set me on a path of running with no destination, at least none that I could discern at the time. It took me a long time to slow down and think. I might never have slowed down if it hadn't been for the sinking of the *Trashman*.

A savvy kid, I quickly learned that animals and nature were much more predictable than people. So I spent much of my youth in the wilds of Texas exploring, building forts, collecting dying or abandoned critters and caring for them. When I was old enough, I sought out the wilds of the world. By plane, boat, train, bus, or on foot—it didn't matter as long as I was moving from adventure to adventure. I raced sailboats, backpacked, hiked, skied, fished, hunted, smoked, and drank. In the process, I made a few friends, and I always kept my commitments brief. But I liked it that way. It was safer, mentally and physically.

The distinctly defined survival skills I had learned at an early age became an integral part of the lessons that, right or wrong, good or bad, accompanied me well into my young adult years, up until the very moment we sank in the Atlantic Ocean. From the day the *Trashman* went down to the day we were rescued, I knew I could survive. Again, I had found my place in the wild. Nature was brutal, but nature was also honest.

I can't blame my mother, of course. The environment she was born into was even crazier than the one I was brought up in. She had spent her childhood trying to survive her father. He set her on the path of running, and I was baggage she just couldn't manage to carry. That fact set me on my own path of running, and the pattern no doubt goes back generations. How far back it goes, where it started, is not important. What is important is that it stopped—with me. I survived it. I managed to grow, and most importantly, I managed to keep it from poisoning my own children.

My mother was sexually abused by her father, but without extensive help, without the will to examine her own life, growth and healing were not available to her. There was no way she could learn to be a nurturing mother, a whole person.

Despite my mother's behavior, despite how psychologically abusive she was to me, when she sent me away for good, I desperately missed her. I can only imagine what her life must have been like as a child to make her the way she was.

And to give credit where it's due, I can see now that a large part of her behavior was her just trying to survive. When she whisked me and Lee away to Vail, Colorado, in the middle of the night, she was merely adapting to a scary situation: Her husband was coming back to kill her. She could just as easily have been in denial, and we all might have wound up the victims of just one more shooting in the Bermuda Triangle of Texas. It happens all the time.

I seemed to have developed an irresistible drive toward an unattainable goal. Ultimately, being on that path would come ever closer to taking my life. And then miraculously, it would allow me to take it back and build it into the life I now have, a life I could scarcely imagine, let alone reach, back then.

Watching the last foot of the *Trashman* disappear beneath the sea, I knew my existence would never be the same. Once again the lure of adventure had enticed me against my better judgment. Just like a heroin addict looking for the ultimate fix, I had finally gone too far, overdosing on my drug of choice, adrenaline.

It's exciting to be afraid. I had learned that as a child, managed it and mastered it against my will. But that passion, carried into adulthood, that living on the edge—surfing the waves of danger to cheat the devil one more time—almost cost me my life. Against all odds, at the age of twenty-four, I had survived yet again, but the cost this time was too high. Would I ever survive surviving? Could I ever heal completely? Could I get back into the ordinary world?

Viktor Frankl, a psychiatrist, was imprisoned by the Nazis in Auschwitz and Dachau for three years during World War II. In his book, *Man's Search for Meaning*, he writes,

> In the final analysis it becomes clear that the sort of person the prisoner becomes was the result of an inner decision, and not the result of camp influences alone. Fundamentally, therefore, any man can, even under such circumstances, decide what shall become of him—mentally and spiritually.

For all practical purposes, my life had only just begun the day I was rescued from the Atlantic Ocean. Initially I wanted to crawl in a hole away from all the insufferable and painful memories. I hated the Coast Guard for leaving us out there. I hated myself for going in the first place. I hated my mother for my lost childhood. And, I was angry with God. In addition, I felt a tremendous amount of guilt for crawling into my hole and not being more appreciative of the grizzly death I had been spared, the beautiful miracle of the life I was being offered.

Over and over I replayed the crazy events of life. Over and over my gut told me to be thankful for my miracle of survival. It was like a tiny spark in the very depths of my dark soul. And soon I began to realize the magnitude of what had happened to me. Not just the sinking but my whole insane life—I had been to places where few people had ever gone. I had felt the evaporation of the self in the presence of God. I no longer feared death. And, although I was the most unlikely of messengers, I had a job to do. God had told me in Meg's last dying word to "tell." I was a survivor. No matter how hard it was, I had to get up and shake the dust off. I had to keep my miracle of life alive. I had to let the world know that the most important lessons we learn come wrapped in very funky paper.

It was to be a long road for me, but some people never get there. At least I'm here to tell about it, and that, rather than running, has become my main goal in life: To pass on what I've learned from these extraordinary experiences. Because I see them all now as opportunities for spiritual growth. I don't in any way look back and blame anyone—most especially not my mother. When I look back, I see all those people caught in the same web of insanity, unable to get out on their own because they simply couldn't see it themselves. Their lives were unexamined and destined to remain so. It would take something enormous and catastrophic to blow apart their lives in order for them to reflect objectively on what they themselves have been doing.

For most of us, nothing that big ever happens, so we muddle along, hurting ourselves and others. For the very rich, money and power can insulate them from those catastrophes and from the need to examine their lives. People literally get away with murder and simply go on doing what they've always done. But money could never heal their souls.

My case was different. Something enormous and catastrophic *did* blow apart my life and force me to examine it.

Many of us use our suffering or the injustices we experience as excuses for our failures, for our inadequacies, for our inability to cope. But we have a huge choice in the matter: We can refuse to be victims and turn ourselves into rescuers instead. That's what I've chosen to be.

ten

The Ten Lessons for Survival

When I was thirteen years old, my mother looked at me very seriously one day and said, "Debbie, you need to realize one thing in life: no one gives a damn about you but yourself. And don't you ever forget it." I never did.

Years later, when I moved back to Fort Worth as an adult, people would come up to me on the street and say, "I can't believe you survived your childhood." I can: I did it by learning survival skills at a very early age. I learned to trust my intuition: When bad things were happening, I sensed it early and believed it quickly. I honed an acute awareness of what was going on around me, and I was always ready to adapt to the situation at hand. I learned to take advantage of the rare bits of luck that came my way and use them to the fullest. I kept myself motivated with a vision of the future—that happy life I'd have someday—and that strengthened my will to live. I learned to make choices as if my life depended on it, because it did. I knew one day I'd be accountable for the choices I'd made. I sought God's grace as well as my own inner grace, which I knew would keep me balanced. I worked and worked on forgiveness, and I'm still working. And most of all, I learned that I was on my own and had to take care of myself.

Of course, I wasn't completely aware of any of those things at the time. In fact, it's taken me my whole life to recognize them, own them, and give them the respect they're due. But those simple lessons, which I started learning as a small child, have brought me here, to the life I'd always dreamed of having, filled with love and happiness.

So the good news is: This story has a happy ending. The even better news is that anyone can learn the lessons that led me here. These lessons can be summarized in the following words:

1. Awareness
2. Intuition
3. Luck and Timing
4. Preparation
5. Adaptability
6. Vision
7. Will
8. Accountability
9. Forgiveness
10. Grace

1. Awareness

Consciously knowing what's going on around you can keep you out of trouble. Children know this from birth. They are paying serious attention to their surroundings, rapidly and naturally sorting out what's good and bad in their environment—and letting you know their decisions in no uncertain terms. But the art of paying attention—and believing the evidence of your senses—is gradually lost to us because of the increasing complexity of our needs and environment.

From bad music in grocery stores to the roar of traffic, we learn to tune out what we perceive as meaningless or unimportant. We do it out of self-protection—otherwise we'd be overwhelmed by sensory information—but it can be a dangerous habit. In order to survive, we need to relearn the lesson that children know: To pay conscious attention so we can avoid the stuff that could hurt us.

This is something that's easy to practice every day: Simplify and streamline. Stop multitasking. When you're driving on the freeway, tailgating another car while talking on your cell phone and drinking a latte, stop and ask yourself: What am I doing? What are the risks? Is it worth it? Then reduce the number of things you have to concentrate on to the most vital. (Hint: That's driving the car; the latte and the conversation can wait.) By freeing your mind from subsidiary demands, you can now fully concentrate on the most important. Now stop the tailgating.

Awareness works on two levels: first by keeping in mind the big picture of a situation (I am driving a car. I am freezing in a rubber dinghy.), and second by looking at the details of the environment for clues that potentially threaten or support that big picture (My cell phone is ringing. There's seaweed floating by that could keep me warm.).

By making awareness a part of everyday life, we have a better chance of noticing when something big goes wrong, whether it's discovering a lump that wasn't there yesterday or seeing a wall of black clouds approaching on the horizon.

2. Intuition

Listening to your gut can save your life. From the moment I met John Lippoth, the captain of the *Trashman*, I knew something was wrong. My intuition told me, but I didn't listen, and it nearly cost me my life.

Scientists are now finding that "gut feelings" or intuition is not just imaginary. We are constantly taking in information that we're not registering on a conscious level. This information becomes part of our decision-making apparatus, seated in a part of the brain that is normally beyond our conscious awareness. But by paying attention to gut feelings and analyzing them, we can bring them into awareness and let them guide us.

My friend Yossi Ghinsberg was lost in the Bolivian jungle for seventeen days and nearly died. At the age of twenty-one, Yossi had joined a group of explorers for a hiking and rafting adventure in South America. But he sensed that the leader was mentally unbalanced in the same way I'd sensed that John Lippoth was. Like me, Yossi went anyway and nearly lost his life, facing everything from jaguars to flooding rivers to quicksand.

We get our information about what's good and bad in the world through the conscious world of the senses as well as through the unconscious world of intuition. Learning to use it can save our lives.

3. Luck and Timing

Both gifts and threats arise at random in our environment. It's precisely because we can't plan for or count on them, that we see them as examples of good or bad luck and timing. *We* assign them meaning; they have none on their own. So the trick is to be constantly on the alert for them, and to keep a positive outlook that allows you to take advantage of them.

We had an amazing piece of luck and timing at work for us in the sinking of the *Trashman*. Out of thirty-five hundred miles of open water, we happened to sink in the only fifty-five-mile-wide patch where the water was warm. If we'd sunk outside the Gulf Stream, where the water temperature was in the fifties, we'd have quickly succumbed to hypothermia and died.

We still had to deal with the sharks and complete lack of emergency supplies, however.

Life gives you breaks, but they are usually slim advantages, not great and sudden victories. To make use of luck and timing, we must *prepare*, so that we're ready to make use of those little advantages. That's the next lesson I learned.

4. Preparation

I was not technically or specifically prepared to survive a sinking when the *Trashman* went down. In fact, without life vests, survival rations, and so on, I was embarrassingly *un*prepared. But in another sense, I was more than ready for the wrenching emotional and mental test of the *Trashman* because of what I'd been through during my childhood.

Preparation then is both conscious and unconscious, and its manifestations are both physical and mental. You can have all the equipment in the world for coping with a disaster at sea, but if you don't have the right mental conditioning, it will count for nothing: Look at what happened to Mark when he lost the life raft.

Having the proper material and equipment on hand for an emergency is the easy part. In the survival kit I describe at the end of this book, I talk about the material things we need.

The mental, spiritual, and emotional preparation is a bit more elusive, but it is achievable. Much of the preparation involves the other nine lessons, particularly learning to give up blaming others and learning to take responsibility for ourselves. Vitally important too is believing and accepting the fact that bad things can and will happen, even in our overprotected world.

Another step is learning techniques for controlling emotion: People who panic or who give in to fits of anger under the slightest stress have a lot of work to do before they can expect to be calm in a real emergency. And calm is a vital component of preparedness. Spiritual practices, such as prayer or meditation, can really help in this regard.

I can't overemphasize the importance of being prepared inside yourself to meet an emergency. Get the stuff you need, of course, but be sure your mind and heart are ready to face the worst. Because as I've learned, even if you don't have the proper physical equipment, having the right mindset and attitude can carry you through.

5. Adaptability

Adapting means being willing and able to change your plans in the face of new information. Tenacity and stick-to-it-iveness are wonderful qualities in their way, but you'll note that I don't include them in my "top ten" survival lessons. That's because stubbornly insisting on staying the course when the course is becoming increasingly ill-advised is no virtue in my book. Inflexible adherence to patterns of behavior that obviously don't work (running away, bulimia, to name two) determined a lot of my life—and was the stuff of many of my mistakes.

The flip side of rigidity is adaptability, being flexible, going with the flow, changing with changing situations. And believe me, all situations change, and your responses to them have to move as quickly as they do.

Adaptability is making lemonade when you've got lemons, rather than insisting on orange juice. It's about taking what's there and working with it. It ties in with awareness, because it's about seeing clearly what's in front of you, and it can lead to true creativity and innovation, because it's about tailoring what is to what could be.

Be adaptable. Don't let your biases get the better of you. Keep an open mind, and be alert to new opportunities. That's good advice for surviving an ordinary day, too.

6. Vision

When trouble comes—and it eventually comes to us all—we either survive it or give up. What makes the difference?

To survive, we have to have an aiming point, a goal, a reason to go forward. We have all seen people who simply give up in the face of real crisis. Those are the people who have no vision of the future—a future that includes them. They have not figured out the purpose of their lives.

Doctors see this all the time with cancer patients. Two patients may have the exact same diagnosis and prognosis. One gives up, while the other fights fiercely and survives. Lance Armstrong is a perfect example of someone with a vision of the future. No one thought he could beat the cancer he had, which had spread to his brain. But he was so focused on getting back on his bike and winning the Tour de France that he powered his way through. He had a purpose in life. Similarly, no one thought it was possible to win that race seven times. His vision of the future made that possible, too.

Knowing what's possible (note that I didn't say probable, because that doesn't enter into it) is extremely important. It opens the door to hope. And hope is nothing more than a clear vision of the future. In 1952, for example, people said that it was impossible for a human being to run a mile in four minutes. It was accepted wisdom, and some doctors even claimed that it would kill you if you tried.

Then an Englishman man named Roger Bannister beat the mark by four-tenths of a second. Suddenly, people all over the world began running a mile in less than four minutes. Obviously, human physiology hadn't changed overnight. What had changed was that they *now knew it was possible*. And that belief, that hope, that vision of success, released them and the power they had within them to run faster.

Sitting in that dinghy, my vision was to get home and make peace with my mother—and make hell for the Coast Guard. Maybe these weren't the most elevated or universal goals, maybe I should have wanted to come home and cure cancer or something. But my vision was persistent, strong, and true. I knew what I wanted, and I clearly saw a future in which I would get what I wanted. And then I got to live an even better future.

7. Will

Will grows directly out of our vision of the future and how passionate we are about our purpose in life. This is where the tenacity I talked about before really belongs, not in clinging tenaciously to the small stuff, but in holding tight, firm, and fast to life itself. To loving life.

My motto is "No victims, only survivors. Have passion for life." It is that passion that fuels the will to live. And the more passionate you are about life—the people in it, the things you love to do—the stronger your will to live will be when you're challenged to survive.

This means creating a passion-driven life. Hate your job? Do something else. Think you're trapped? Look at Tish in the preface of this book or Yossi in the Bolivian jungle or the millions made homeless by Katrina. Look around you: There are miracles everywhere. Go get yourself one. Believe me, you're going to need it one day.

As with vision, your passion needn't be extraordinary. You could love to climb mountains or adore needlepoint. It doesn't matter *what* turns you on—it only matters that *something* does. Because that something will power you, keep you lively, keep you interested, keep you involved. Keep you here.

8. Accountability

We will all answer for our choices. This is not the same as saying we'll be judged. It means that our choices have consequences, and we must accept and deal with them. You go out in the rain without an umbrella, you'll get wet: your choice, inevitable consequence.

By thinking this way, by knowing that we will be held accountable, we can actually begin to make better choices.

Viktor Frankl writes, "It did not really matter what we expected from life, but rather what life expected from us." Frankl believed that life was questioning us all the time, and that "Our answer must consist, not in talk and meditation, but in right action and right conduct. Life ultimately means taking the responsibility to find the right answers to its problems and fulfill the tasks which it constantly sets for each individual."

I try to do this all the time in my everyday life, simply by asking myself a series of questions about the choices I'm about to make: What is the worst that can happen if I make this choice badly? What is the reward if I make it well? How big is the risk I'm willing to take for that reward? Have I prepared myself well to make this choice? Do I know all I need to know? In making this choice, am I taking into account the others it might benefit or harm?

9. Forgiveness

George Eliot writes, "Deep unspeakable suffering may well be called a baptism, a regeneration, the initiation into a new state." And Helen Keller writes, "Character cannot be developed in ease and quiet. Only through experience of trial and suffering can the soul be strengthened, vision cleared, ambition inspired, and success achieved."

All of us suffer. But it is how we react to the source of our suffering that determines whether we are vengeful or forgiving, whether the experience diminishes us or enables us to grow. If we blame others for our suffering, we make ourselves victims.

(It's your fault I'm in this mess.) If we forgive others and nature and even God—if we embrace suffering and use it as an opportunity to grow—then we are free to be survivors and even rescuers. (I'm in a mess, and I can get out.) Leaving out the blame leaves room for growth.

Hermann Hesse writes, "Love your suffering. Do not resist it, do not flee from it. It is your aversion that hurts, nothing else."

Being angry can give you the momentary power you need to push through. The body is wired to give us that burst of energy. My anger at the Coast Guard helped sustain me through five days without food or water. But staying angry and unforgiving over long periods of time simply wears us down.

The art of forgiveness is worth learning. Sometimes it takes decades, as it did in my case, but we can always try in little ways each day. Learning to let go of the little things—the guy who cuts you off in traffic, the rude clerk, the customer service rep who puts you on hold for forever—is a small but real step. Do you stew on those things, thinking up great comeback lines? Or do you simply say: That's the way the world is. Get on with it.

Marcus Aurelius, one of the great Stoic philosophers, writes, "If you are distressed by anything external, the pain is not due to the thing itself, but to your estimate of it; and this you have the power to revoke at any moment."

Use the power: Forgive and set yourself free.

10. Grace

There are a lot of different definitions of grace, and a lot of different words used by others to express what I call grace. No wonder: This is a tough concept.

What I mean by grace is a sense of oneness with your surroundings, a merging of you with everything. It's not submitting to fate, but embracing it. It's not giving up or giving in, but just giving. It's not surrendering, but it is surrender.

Grace is the state you achieve when you've gone through the survival journey, when you've been tested and have embraced the test and have learned from it. It releases you to a place of joy and acceptance.

In his famous book, *Flow*, Mihaly Csikszentmihalyi has a chapter called "Cheating Chaos," which reminds me of this state of grace. In fact, I think that what I call grace is what he calls flow. He sets out four simple rules for transforming a bad experience—or any experience—into a gracious experience:

1. Set goals.
2. Become immersed in the activity.
3. Pay attention.
4. Learn to enjoy your immediate experience.

"When adversity threatens to paralyze us," he writes, "we need to reassert control by finding a new direction in which to invest psychic energy, a direction that lies outside the reach of external forces." That sounds very much like what Viktor Frankl says about a person's internal state not being dictated by his environment: "He may retain his human dignity even in a concentration camp. Dostoevski said once, 'There is only one thing that I dread: not to be worthy of my sufferings.'"

When Alexander Solzhenitsyn was imprisoned in a gulag, he said that at the worst of times he sometimes "felt such a rush of rhymes and images that I seemed to be wafted overhead…

At such moments I was both free and happy… For me there was no barbed wire… I was actually away on a distant flight." Clearly he had achieved a state of grace and transcendence, despite his horrible surroundings.

Such experiences may be difficult to understand for people who have not had them. But if we believe them and regard them as possible, then in the crush of our worst experiences, they can help us face literally anything.

The great irony of survival is that none of us are getting out alive. Our physical presence here on earth is terminal. So why put so much effort into survival? Why not get the inevitable over with? Why bother to learn the lessons? In part, the answer is: To have a life well lived. To die well we must have lived well and not have given up.

Viktor Frankl writes of ministering to a woman who was dying in the concentration camp. She told him, "I am grateful that fate has hit me so hard. In my former life I was spoiled and did not take spiritual accomplishments seriously." She had achieved a state of grace because she had truly and fully experienced life now. That is the point of the struggle. And in that struggle, you never know when life is going to give you one more chance.

I have a friend named Allison whom I think exemplifies the lessons I've learned and presents a good model for others to ponder.

About a decade ago, Janet, Allison's one-year-old child, started to get picky about food. Allison shrugged it off as a phase, until Janet, after eating birthday cake at a party, began projectile vomiting in the car on the way home. Allison assumed it was a bug, but Janet's symptoms over the following weeks worsened. She developed diarrhea and vomited constantly. She became frightened, tearful, and lethargic. Then she stopped walking, and Allison knew this was no ordinary childhood illness.

The pediatrician suggested it could be giardia, usually contracted through a contaminated water supply. Allison lived in a metropolitan area with a perfectly good water supply; she knew it wasn't giardia.

Janet dropped seven pounds and began to exhibit signs of muscle wasting. Allison combed the medical literature for clues, and found that her daughter had all ten symptoms of Celiac disease, an autoimmune response that makes people intolerant of gluten, which is in many of the major grains we eat. (Wheat, rye, and barley aren't referred to as the staff of life for nothing: they're in almost all common foods; read the labels!) Left untreated, Celiac disease can progress to grave illness, and trigger other autoimmune diseases and even death.

The pediatrician doubted such a "rare" diagnosis (it occurs in 1 out of every 133 people of the population). But Allison knew in her gut that she was right. She took Janet to a pediatric gastroenterologist, who suggested the same diagnosis, but cautioned against treatment until testing proved the disease.

Weeks of treating symptoms followed; no medicines helped. Finally, with Thanksgiving approaching and no conclusion reached, Allison demanded an intestinal biopsy, which she knew from her reading was the only way to diagnose Celiac with any certainty. The biopsy came back positive.

Unfortunately, the nutritionist sent to advise Allison knew little about Celiac, and Janet was still not gaining weight. Once again, Allison took matters into her own hands. Using the then-relatively new Internet, she located a support group in California and contacted another mom whose child had Celiac disease. Remembers Allison, "She said to go buy a bag of corn chips and let Janet eat as much as she wanted." The corn wouldn't hurt Janet the way the wheat had, and it would satisfy her hunger and give her the big jolt of calories she needed. "That's what my daughter lived on for three weeks. She gained weight. She stopped vomiting. She got better."

Allison began adding fruits and vegetables and meat to Janet's diet and watched her grow robust and round-cheeked again. Janet is eleven now, a strong, healthy, and happy girl. She and her mother have worked hard together to figure out how to live in a world where most foods could literally kill her.

Today, she makes light of it all. "I've known people who've had to watch their children go through chemotherapy. No, we're the lucky ones," she says.

Allison saved her daughter's life, and she did it with the ten lessons for survival. She paid attention to signs and symptoms, trusted her intuition, did her homework, and fortuitously used all resources to hand. When one doctor and diagnosis failed her, she found another. She took full responsibility for her actions, even when she went up against established medical wisdom. She was determined throughout that her child was not going to die, and she refused to rest until she had answers. In her and Janet's coping with the disease, there was no bitterness against an unfair fate, but only sweet acceptance.

Life is a miracle. Thriving in life is all about making lemonade out of lemons and always seeing that the resulting glass of lemonade is, at the very least, half full.

You and you alone must take responsibility for surviving and thriving in life: No one else can do it for you. When you find yourself in a questionable situation, STOP:

- Be still and give your spirit a chance to do its job. Become aware of your surroundings; look for the obstacles and the opportunities.
- Listen to your intuition, the innate mechanism that guides you and warns you.
- Accept those moments when the universe offers up a little luck and good timing. Always be prepared; as Marie Curie put it, "Chance favors the prepared mind."
- Be willing to change old patterns and beliefs at a moment's notice.
- Always hold onto your vision of the future, and never give up.
- Remember that you and only you are responsible for your survival and your happiness. Your choices are just that, choices, and you will be held accountable for them.
- Learn to forgive, and be thankful for the time you have on earth, because life is an adventure and an incredible, albeit sometimes difficult, journey.

Commentary

by Laurence Gonzales

When I wrote *Deep Survival*, I used Debbie's story of being cast away at sea as an example because I thought it was an excellent illustration of how an ordinary person can come through extraordinary circumstances. At the time, I had no idea what an extraordinary life she'd led. When I learned the story of her childhood, I was doing research for a new book, which I've been calling "Everyday Survival," because it deals with the challenges faced, not by adventurers at sea or in the mountains or the wilderness, but in everyday life, from cancer to divorce to business crisis. It deals with human behavior and attempts to illuminate some of its baffling mysteries.

Some of the most difficult challenges in life are those faced by children in dysfunctional families. A child has not had a broad range of experiences on which to build an emotional system to sustain him- or herself. Children are left to depend on their innate survival abilities far more than are adults, who have developed over time into survivors, or victims, through their experiences. But even someone like Debbie—seemingly a "born" survivor—suffers greatly from what she went through as a child.

When a child is rejected by her mother, or even ignored, it can be fatal. I'm not being dramatic or speaking figuratively here. There's a famous case study that demonstrates this fact. After World War II, there were thousands of orphans in Europe and England, and therefore many orphanages and hospitals to care for them. In one hospital, the doctors ordered that the children be fed and changed regularly and kept warm but forbade anyone to interact with them or hold them. The theory was that this would prevent them from being exposed to infection. They had nourishing food and good clothing. They were warm and safe. And they all died.

In fact, this "experiment," if you can call it that, had been tried before. Frederick II, the Holy Roman emperor of southern Italy, wanted to know what the natural human language was. If no one spoke to a baby, what language would it speak? The emperor decided to find out. He had some newborn children sequestered. They were bathed, fed, clothed, and kept warm, but no one was allowed to speak to them or play with them. They all died too. As the monk who kept records at the time explained, "the children could not live without clappings of the hands, and gestures, and gladness of countenance, and blandishments."

Robert Sapolsky, a MacArthur fellow and author of the book *Why Zebras Don't Get Ulcers*, described an unintentional experiment in Germany after the Second World War. There were two nurses at two different orphanages. Fräulein Grun was warm and nurturing. Fräulein Schwartz was cold and stiff. The babies at Fräulein Grun's orphanage thrived and grew. Those at Fräulein Schwartz's did not. When Fräulein Schwartz was transferred to Fräulein Grun's orphanage, the children there stopped growing—and the ones at the place she had left started growing again. Sapolsky writes,

> Until recent decades, being placed in an orphanage was one of the most dangerous events that could happen to a child. In 1915, despite adequate food and health care, the majority of orphanages in the United States had close to 100 percent mortality rates. Even some thirty years later, a third of infants in orphanages were still dying, 'in spite of good food and meticulous medical care.'

In light of this, it's amazing that not only Debbie but also her mother were able to survive the neglect and brutality of their infancy and early childhood.

Despite the overwhelming evidence against the idea, psychologists in the 1950s still believed that all behavior was shaped by reward and punishment. If a rat could be taught to run a maze by putting food pellets at the end, then so could a human. If a rat could be kept from behaving in a certain way by giving it an electric shock, then human behavior could be shaped by punishment as well. Pediatricians and psychologists told parents never to pick up a child who was crying because it would "spoil" him. The theory was that infants become attached to their mothers because mothers are the source of reward: Food from breast milk. Nothing more, nothing less. And rewarding them for crying by giving them affection would simply encourage more crying.

Sapolsky writes,

> Something roughly akin to love is needed for proper biological development, and its absence is among the most aching, distorting stressors that we can suffer. Scientists, physicians, and other caregivers have often been dim at recognizing its importance in the mundane biological processes of organs and tissues growing and developing. Yet young organisms were able to teach this fact to surprised scientists in a classic set of studies conducted in the 1950s through the 1970s, studies that are, in my opinion, among the most haunting and troubling of all the pages of science.

He's referring to, among others, the work of a psychologist named Harry Harlow, who conducted a famous experiment that began to change people's minds. Harlow isolated a baby monkey and gave it two fake mothers. One was made of wire and had a nipple that gave it milk—the reward. The other was made of cloth but gave no milk—it gave only comfort. The monkey drank the milk from the wire mother, but spent all the rest of his time curled up with the cloth mother. He even hid behind it, not the wire one, when frightened.

Milk, like the money Debbie's family had, means little without love. And without love, you'll attach yourself to almost anything that vaguely resembles it. This can lead you into some really bad choices later in life. You may marry the wrong person or get on the wrong boat. Such choices may cost you your life, as Debbie knows: Bad choices almost killed her.

But there's more: In the 1980s, psychologist Mary Ainsworth showed that the way a mother treats a child predicts what kind of emotional life, what kinds of survival skills, that child will have as an adult. If a mother is responsive, affectionate, caring, and predictable, the child will grow up to be secure and successful. Such mothers pay attention to their babies and sense when they want to be picked up or fed or left alone, and respond accordingly. Children of caring mothers grow up to be socially successful, competent in school, secure, and happy. If the mother is unaffectionate, angry, or rigid, the child will grow up to be insecure and indifferent. And if a mother is erratic in her behavior and insecure herself, the child too will grow up to be needy, socially awkward, and highly sensitive, with no self-confidence.

In Debbie's case, her mother was a combination of the unaffectionate, angry mother and the erratic one. Debbie was insecure and needy enough to attach herself to the wrong people both in love and in sailing. She was also deprived enough to need the false comfort that addictive behavior brought through her bulimia. But she had a deep-seated, inborn strength that kept her afloat, kept her fighting, and there has been precious little research done to learn where this ability comes from. Even among our nearest primate cousins, the great apes, there are clear divisions between the born survivors and the born victims, and, like people, they pass these traits down from mother to daughter.

The mother's emotional system organizes that of the child through a complex set of subtle signals from facial expression to smell. Myron Hofer, a psychiatrist and researcher at Columbia University, showed how the mother's body warmth and smell control how active an infant is. Her touch stimulates growth hormone. Her breast milk and how often she gives it control heart rate and sleeping patterns. Without knowing or intending anything, a mother exerts a profound influence on how her baby develops everything from bone structure to attention levels. Without the mother's attention, the baby's physiological and emotional systems literally fall apart.

In *Deep Survival*, I wrote that the emotional system can be thought of as an extension of the immune system—something that tells us what defines us and what constitutes everything else in the world—and whether those things we encounter out there are good or bad for us. In fact, I learned after writing the book that Dr. Candace B. Pert, a researcher at Georgetown University Medical Center in Washington, D.C., says that the emotional system really *is* part of the immune system. Whatever disrupts the emotions destroys immune function and blurs the boundary between us and the outside world, opening us to infections, either physical or emotional. And numerous researchers have shown that powerful negative emotions, or any prolonged stress, can make you sick. In some cases, it can kill you. The numerous times Debbie fell gravely ill, from adult chicken pox to spinal meningitis, are examples of this.

But these destructive processes don't have to kill you directly. They can weaken and confuse you and leave you desperately searching for the thing that's missing in your life. They can scramble the emotional part of your brain that detects danger and reward, and that in turn can lead you to make foolish choices and mistakes, ones that may eventually get you killed. That's what happened to Debbie.

This is not the same thing as blaming the parents for the faults of the children. It goes much deeper than that, because parents who wreak havoc on a child's emotional system have already survived their own emotional havoc. There's no way to know how far back it goes. But by knowing about it, by recognizing it, by discussing it, we can be better equipped to stop it so that it doesn't go any further—to our children and grandchildren.

But when your emotional system is out of balance, sometimes no amount of thinking can save you. A phenomenon known as "inattentional blindness" can actually prevent us from seeing what's right in front of us.

In a now-famous experiment at Harvard, a group of psychologists showed a video of basketball players passing the ball and asked people to count the number of passes made by each team. So intent were the subjects on their task, they did not notice when a woman with an umbrella or a person dressed in a gorilla costume (there were two versions of the video) walked into the action and stayed there for about five seconds. The researchers noted that "Thirty-five percent of the observers failed to notice the woman with the umbrella, even though her presence was obvious to anyone not engaged in the counting task." Fifty-six percent didn't notice the gorilla.

This inattentional blindness is pervasive and stems from the way we create models of the world. For the most part, we don't really *see* the world around us; rather, we create models that make it simpler to get around in life. Some of those models concern the way things look. You can find a familiar object in a jumble of junk in a drawer because you have a stable mental model of its appearance. Other models are what we call "muscle memory," such as knowing how to tie your shoes without thinking about it. Still others embody rules about how the world works—gravity, for example. If a magician makes a caged tiger levitate off the stage floor, it's surprising, because it violates a trusted model: Heavy objects fall down, they don't rise up.

These various models are useful and necessary. Without them, we'd never get anything done, because we'd constantly have to figure out—all over again—everything they represent. But in their very convenience lies the possibility that they will blind us to changes taking place around us. If we can miss a gorilla on a basketball court, think of all the other things we must certainly be missing every day.

That's why Debbie's first five lessons—awareness, intuition, luck and timing, preparation, and adaptability—are so relevant: It is only by paying careful attention, by examining our own lives and the assumptions we make, by updating our mental models as the world changes around us, that we can avoid the trap of blindness.

Certain types of emotional trauma in childhood can make it much more difficult to maintain that kind of awareness. They can distort not only our models of the world but our model of ourselves as well.

A child is a living organism, built to survive. One of the key elements of survival is defining what is you and what is not—having boundaries. That's essentially what your immune system does, too: It identifies what's you and what's not and tries to kill invading organisms, such as bacteria that might make you sick. When you're a child, your emotional system is also set up to define what's good and bad in the environment and to help you get what you need and avoid what could hurt you. It helps maintain those boundaries between what's you and what's not.

When an adult violates a child's boundaries, it sets in motion a complete disruption of all the natural systems that protect and nourish that child. When an adult has sex with a child or is violent to a child, physically or psychologically, it deprives the child of an essential ingredient of survival: Control over personal boundaries. And that's how Debbie found herself in Annapolis about to take the voyage of her life: She had lost her boundaries and had given up control to others she knew she couldn't trust. She was as vulnerable as if she'd lost her skin. And she watched it all happening as if she'd been split in two.

We live in a culture that prizes independence. We assume we can go it on our own. But all the research in this field in the past fifty years says this view is wrong. People need other people. And children especially need their mothers. They need them to be predictable and stable and supportive. This means, in short, that a parent needs to respond to the child—not control, direct, intimidate, or coerce the child into doing the parent's will.

In a strange way, Debbie's experiences as a child both led her to calamity and saved her from it when it arrived. The very adversity that set her up for disaster helped shape the person and personality that were up to the challenge of surviving it. There is a deep lesson in that for all of us: Cherish your misfortune and learn from it. For whatever brought you there may be the gift that gets you out.

When Debbie was little and her world became too chaotic, too frightening, to handle, she hid herself and prayed. Prayer is a repetitive activity that focuses the mind, the will, the emotions, the attention.

In fact, neuroscientists have seen that rhythmic, ritual activities calm the emotions. They have a physiologically calming effect on the brain and can take you completely out of yourself at times. There is evidence for this from primitive cultures, where dancing, drumming, singing, and other rituals are used to induce transcendental states; and there is more evidence for this from great religious mystics. Andrew Newberg is an M.D. researcher at the University of Pennsylvania who has spent years studying what goes on in the brain during religious experiences. He found that an area of the brain called the parietal lobe was quieted during these experiences, which could be brought on by rhythmic rituals such as prayer, meditation, and dancing. The parietal lobe is the area of the brain that gives us a sense of self, the limits of our own bodies and their position in three-dimensional space. During religious or mystical experiences, this parietal area is turned off, so to speak, producing a sense of oneness with the universe, a sense of God. In fact, the parietal lobe is turned off during orgasm, too. Without knowing it, Debbie, even as a child, was calming herself by suppressing the activity in this brain area.

She did it again when the *Trashman* sank. She hid under the spray skirt in the bow to separate herself from the madness of the crew (who so resembled her family—people she'd learned to be attracted to), and she repeated the Lord's Prayer over and over and over. When John and Mark were eaten by sharks, prayer and meditation were her lifeline, her tools to keep her from going over the edge—and perhaps over the side to join her shipmates. Early in life, she had developed a strategy for transforming her inner space when she had no control of the world around her. And in this sense, she had the qualities that Viktor Frankl describes in those who survived the chaos and terror of Auschwitz.

When Debbie wrote her account of the sinking of the *Trashman*, much of the scientific research that would help explain the crew's actions, reactions, and perceptions had either not yet been done or was very new. For example, *The Emotional Brain* by Joseph LeDoux wasn't published until 1996, two years after Debbie's book came out under the title *Albatross*.[1] LeDoux's work showed how specialized areas of our brain that make up our emotional responses and direct our behavior can take over in an emergency, forcing us to stop thinking and simply react. In some cases, this is good, such as when you duck away from a falling object to protect yourself. In a survival emergency, those automated emotional responses can betray us, too, as when her shipmate, Mark, inflated the life raft in a panic before tethering it to the ship. The fact that it blew away, leaving them without survival supplies, resulted in the death of both Mark and John, and nearly killed the rest of the crew, too.

In such situations, your emotional system can literally stop you from thinking. The thinking brain, the neocortex, still does its work. But the much stronger emotional brain, the limbic system, is more powerful and keeps pushing you toward your fate. When Debbie joined the crew of the *Trashman* against her better judgment, that's the struggle she was engaged in: Reason versus emotion.

People always ask what kept Debbie going after the sinking, and there are some answers now. For example, a researcher named Martin Seligman has pioneered the concept of learned helplessness. He saw it in laboratory animals. He put dogs in a situation where their efforts did nothing to improve their condition—say they were given an electric shock, no matter

[1]Recently reissued as *The Sinking* (NVOS Publishing, 2006).

what they tried to do to stop it. They learned to become helpless. They'd just lie down and whimper. Even if they were then put in another box where they could jump over a barrier to get away from the shock, they wouldn't even try. This can happen to people, too. They can become helpless in every way, even when people around them can see obvious ways that they could help themselves or improve their lot.

But here's another thing Seligman discovered: While dogs that were raised in the lab became helpless, dogs who came from the pound didn't. They'd had rough-and-tumble lives, but they had also learned that things in their environment were controllable by them. They'd learned to scrap and fight, to hide and negotiate, and so they kept on trying.

In this sense, Debbie is the epitome of a pound puppy. She'd been raised in a very dangerous world and had learned at an early age that she had to do things for herself. She learned to control her environment—by running away and hiding, for example. And when her Grandmother Queenie would hold her while Debbie cried and would tell her that everything was going to be alright, she learned something else: This, too, will pass. Debbie prayed that everything was going to be alright and was told that it would be, and somehow she managed to internalize this and believe it. Those traits helped her endure unimaginable torment.

Seligman and his colleagues also found out that people who are susceptible to learned helplessness become that way by the way they explain bad things to themselves. He writes in *Learned Helplessness*,

> If you believe the cause of your mess is permanent... you will not act to change it. You will not act to improve yourself. If, however,

> you believe the cause is temporary... you can act to change it... If you think about bad things in always's and never's and abiding traits, you have a permanent, pessimistic style. If you think in sometimes's and lately's, you use qualifiers and blame bad events on transient conditions, you have an optimistic style...

Debbie had managed to develop an optimistic style, and it wouldn't let her give up.

Since *Albatross* was published, some research has been done about how people react in extreme emergencies, and there are many parallels to Debbie's experience. For example, when she was awakened from a sound sleep to find the ship rapidly sinking, she described events happening as if in "a terrifying slow-motion dream." As she watched Brad untie the rubber dinghy Zodiac where she would spend the next five days, she saw the scene in exquisite detail, as she writes in her book: "I saw the muscles in his arms as he dug into the iron-hard knots..." Later, as she clung to the Zodiac, she wondered, "Am I really here? Am I really here?" And even though Mark was screaming at the top of his lungs nearby, she reported, "I could still hear Mark screaming, but his voice seemed muffled and far off—as if his head was underwater and the words were bubbling up from below." Her perceptions became extremely sharp: "I could smell rubber and taste salt on my lips. I became keenly aware of the warmth of the water."

In 2004, a study of police officers who had been in shootouts was published, and the reactions of those officers during those life-and-death moments bear a striking resemblance to Debbie's. They all describe time slowing down, vision narrowing, and the sense of some things becoming extremely acute while others are muffled. They describe, for example, actually seeing bullets hit. They can't hear the shots they fire, though the explosions are extremely loud, but they do hear the tinkling of spent cartridges as they hit the pavement. The rush of adrenaline and other chemicals in the face of death creates an extremely surreal view of the world.

It starts with an initial sense of disbelief or denial. Just as Debbie asked, "Am I really here?," most of the police officers also reported a first reaction of disbelief. One said, "I couldn't believe what was happening. I couldn't believe this guy was turning on me with a gun." While some senses were turned up, others were turned down. They noticed a tremendous amount of visual detail, such as a pants leg moving as a bullet went through it. But hearing was muffled: "I really didn't hear anything," said an officer who fired off fourteen rounds in rapid succession. "The short-barrel M-16 is very loud, it's deafening, but I don't remember hearing it… I don't remember ringing in my ears."

They all experienced the collapse of time. One described "watching those bullet holes appearing in slow motion." Another said, "Time started to move really slow." And another: "At that point, things started to move in a little bit of slow motion."

I find these similarities telling, because the officers were highly trained professionals, well prepared to meet a life-and-death emergency, but Debbie was a twenty-four-year-old girl with no formal training of any sort. Instead, her training had come from her experiences in childhood, when she had been schooled in facing life-and-death situations, including gunfire. In a real yet paradoxical way, the childhood trauma that had led her into catastrophe helped her survive it.

Nevertheless, the repeated surges of stress hormones such as adrenaline and cortisone, starting in infancy, change brain and body chemistry permanently, leaving one vulnerable later in life not only to addiction but to all sorts of other catastrophic choices and accidents. It's not "my mother made me bulimic"; rather, putting a child under constant stress through rejection and abuse causes real, measurable changes in the brain that are associated with patterns of compulsive behavior and bad social decisions. The scientists who study this, such as Antonio Damasio, find that these emotionally abused people behave a lot like people with actual brain damage. (The good news is that the brain is constantly changing, and we can get better.)

Growing up with people who shot each other, drank all the time, and abused children, Debbie didn't develop normal *limbic regulation*, that set of internal cues about what was and wasn't good for her out in the world. When she decided to write a paper for a college class about a dangerous motorcycle gang, for example, she was making a nearly disastrous social choice that stemmed from not having learned to distinguish between good and bad in her environment.

In the same way, joining the crew of the *Trashman* was what scientists call an "intelligent mistake." It involved a kind of denial that is possible if you are well trained from an early age to accept what seems outrageous, to keep coming back to what might hurt you. In one experiment, a rat is trained to run a maze to find food. After it has learned the maze, a barrier is placed halfway to the food. The next time the rat runs the maze, it runs right into the barrier as if it didn't even see it. Scientists call that an "intelligent mistake," because really, the rat's odd behavior in hitting the wall is the result of the hard work that went into learning the maze. We do that all the time in life. And if we're not constantly paying attention to changes in our environment, we're apt to run smack into a new wall someone put up while we weren't looking.

Psychologist John Leach, who studies survival, writes, "When the personality is ripped away there has to be a core remaining to carry the person through… If a person can carry all his support within him then it matters little what the external environment comprises." In those first moments after the sinking, Debbie was finding out what her core was made of.

Near the end of World War II, the U.S.S. *Indianapolis* was torpedoed and sunk, spilling nine hundred sailors into the sea. The Navy botched its rescue almost as badly as the Coast Guard did Debbie's, leaving the sailors stranded for four days before sending help (in the case of the *Trashman*, although the plane had marked its position, the Coast Guard never returned). Doug Stanton's riveting account of the *Indianapolis* in his book *In Harm's Way* leaves no doubt—in my mind, at least—about how important and universal certain principles of survival are and how similar are the reactions of those who refuse to give up.

For example, doing something—anything—to get organized is a key element of survival, whether you're shipwrecked or getting a divorce or battling breast cancer. Floating in the open ocean in a life raft after the sinking of the *Indianapolis*, one sailor decided to clean his pistol. He organized the men in the raft with him to help. Each soldier held one piece of the gun while he disassembled and cleaned it and put it back together. Debbie was trying to do just this sort of thing when she organized the people in her raft to gather seaweed to keep themselves warm. At other times of crisis in her life, she organized herself by going to school or undertaking her conversion to Catholicism.

The sailor who cleaned his pistol was named Giles McCoy, and he was working in other ways to survive a near-hopeless situation. His intuition told him he he'd better do something, and what he came up with was to maintain the only thing he had at hand: his pistol. Luck and timing brought a tin of petroleum jelly floating by amid the wreckage, and McCoy's awareness led him to spot it and pluck it out of the sea to grease his gun. He envisioned a future at home with his family to keep himself motivated and strengthen his will to live. He thought of his mother and her laugh; he loved his mother. He loved his father too, but they had quarreled before he went to sea, and McCoy wanted to get back and make up with him. He didn't want to die on bad terms with his dad. Debbie's situation was the same: she never lost her desire to reconcile with her mother. Such a feeling can provide a very powerful motivation to live, and it can lead a person to take a crucial step away from the bondage of past experience: Forgiveness. Holding a grudge, which is the opposite of forgiveness, takes a huge amount of energy. Unlike anger, which can motivate, holding a grudge creates an internal loop that covers the same ground repeatedly and to no purpose. That loop can be measured through biochemical changes in the brain: It's like driving with the brakes on. Being able to forgive those who have hurt you releases you to focus all your energy for survival.

In his raft, the captain of the U.S.S. *Indianapolis* was also getting organized: He set five-hour watches, kept a makeshift log, and patiently instructed those around him. He kept calm and reassured the young sailors. He asked about their wives or girlfriends and told them about his life, giving them all a sense of something to live for. When they were rescued after four days, these men were able to climb the ladder to the boat and walk under their own power. Many others had to be carried—or worse, had already died.

In other, less well-organized groups, despair set in quickly. The sailors began hallucinating, and some even killed each other in their delirium. Some fell to drinking seawater and went insane. Like Mark and John, they were beset by delusions and swam off in search of some hallucinated salvation (a boat, a hotel, a beach that wasn't there). Sailors from those groups—the ones who didn't die—were too weak to stand after rescue and had to be carried.

In all the cases of survival I have known, the will to live comes from envisioning a future and your own participation in it. It turns out that this is an innate drive of all living things. Even a bacterium envisions a future: It will migrate from one place to another along a line of increasing concentration of nutrients in water, going from a place where there is less nutrient to a place where there is more. Although a bacterium may not have anything we'd call a mental process—an ability to create images—it is behaving as if there is a better future before it. As you move up through the evolutionary levels, that drive toward an imagined future grows more complex and vivid, reaching its peak in humans, who can imagine what's not there, what may seem unlikely ever to be there—and who, clinging to that image, can survive unimaginable hardship.

That future can be anything. It can be the drive to be reunited with a loved one. It can be a need to continue with work about which you're passionate. Viktor Frankl writes in *Man's Search for Meaning* about convincing a scientist in Auschwitz not to commit suicide because he must survive to finish his research. Doug Stanton describes many of the *Indianapolis* crew having this experience. "Many of the survivors," he wrote, "found themselves reaching even deeper inside and summoning a grim refusal to die. No one believed that help was coming, but they tried to convince one another to hang on, as if for the hell of it." At that point, they'd been in the water for three days, and half the original nine hundred sailors were already dead, one every ten minutes or so. And yet, they imagined a future, even when it seemed that help wasn't coming. Debbie did the same.

The point is not that cleaning a gun or standing watch or gathering seaweed helped those people to survive. What helped them was a willingness to continue the struggle, an inner attitude that let them carry on for the sheer, indisputable rightness of staying alive. Willingness is not the same as willfulness. Willfulness is often contrary to reality. Mark was willful and bitter to the end. His rigidity killed him as much as anything. Debbie's willingness to accept the situation she was in and make the most of it allowed her to continue.

Another element in surviving is simply managing and using emotion to sustain oneself. As the days wore on in the drifting Zodiac, Debbie enlisted all manner of emotional states. At one moment, she might need to be motivated, and so she'd think of the Coast Guard and let her anger run wild: She'd see that plane again, dipping out of a cloud to mark her position. They knew where the *Trashman* sank. Why didn't they come? She was desperate to find out why they'd abandoned her. Her anger powered her through to the next stage.

There's nothing new in this strategy. One of the classic stories of survival involves a miner, Pablo, on the Mexican border in 1906 who was lost in the desert while looking for gold. He survived nine days without water (which may be a world record). When he was found, everyone was amazed that he was alive and certain that he wouldn't last the night. But he fought his way back. When he was able to talk, he was asked how he held out. He explained that he believed that his guide had abandoned him so he could get the gold for himself. Pablo was focused on finding him and killing him; that's what kept him alive.

After a bout of anger at the Coast Guard, Debbie might need some moments of quiet, and she'd think of home and live for a while in imagined scenes of green fields and children on swings and dogs barking. Her vivid memories of other environments gave her the strength to come back and face the harsh one in which she found herself. Every successful survivor describes such episodes. A number of Americans who spent years in prison camps during the Vietnam War described their practice of playing golf in their minds. They'd play day after day, modifying the course, selecting their clubs, working on their strategies. It kept them alive.

Everyone is cast away at sea in some sense, at some time of life. It may come in the form of divorce, illness, the loss of a loved one, through natural disaster or war. But no matter how it comes, we must be prepared. Surviving is adaptation, pure and simple. The world will never change to suit us, so we must change to meet it. And then we can have the privilege of looking down on ourselves from a great height and watching the spiritual transformation unfold that will enrich the rest of our lives.

My Survival Kit

I was not physically prepared when the *Trashman* sank. No life jacket, no food, no water, no nothing. I knew there was a life raft in a canister at the stern with all the proper survival gear. But the truth was that I really hadn't thought much about it—at least not until the boat sank and the life raft blew away. The thought of the *Trashman* sinking never entered my mind, so I hadn't prepared. That was one of the toughest lessons I had to learn: *Preparation.*

There are big, scary, equalizing forces out there, both man-made and from Mother Nature. The recent batch—9/11 and the 2004 Asian tsunami, the July 2005 London bombings, Hurricanes Katrina and Rita, the October 2005 bombings in Bali and the earthquake in Pakistan—bring that home loud and clear.

But we'll all have a much better chance of survival if we're just a little bit better prepared mentally, spiritually, and physically.

It's not just me who feels strongly about being prepared. One of my favorite books on the subject is *SAS Survival Handbook: How to Survive in the Wild, in Any Climate, on Land or at Sea*, by John "Lofty" Wiseman (that last name is well deserved), a veteran of the British Army's Special Air Service. This guy is a trained professional survivor, and my paltry stories will never match up to his: he's seen it all. In his book, he writes: "It's crucial that we are prepared for any eventuality and survival training is the best insurance policy you can take out. Just by following the basic techniques, and knowing what to do in an emergency will make the world a safer place."

A healthy body and a strong will to live make a huge difference in the fight for survival. That's what this book is all about. Beyond that, though, knowing how to make—or get—shelter, fire, and water top the "how to survive" list. And for that you need a survival kit.

After years of thinking and reading about this, I have come up with my own version of a survival kit. Most of the items are the basics, but I've added a few extra items for safety as well as pleasure (I need my tea in the morning!). I can fit my entire survival kit into a medium-sized backpack, with room to spare for last-minute essentials (assuming there's time to round them up). Here are my survival kit essentials:

General

- 1 medium-size day backpack, waterproof
- *SAS Survival Handbook* by John "Lofty" Wiseman: *Provides step-by-step directions on how to use almost all of this equipment and MUCH more!*

- Fresh water: *As much as you can reasonably carry; I have included the Nalgene bottles in this list as well as the carabiners to connect them to the outside of the pack*
- 1 or 2 (or 3) Nalgene water bottles
- 1 MSR MiniWorks EX microfilter: *Water filter; keep the directions*
- 2 packages Katadyn Micropur MP1: *Emergency drinking water tablets*
- 2 1-liter collapsible bottles: *I like the Platypus brand*
- 1 small multipurpose flashlight and extra batteries: *Keep the batteries inside, but reverse them in case the light is accidentally turned on (I learned that from "Lofty")*
- 1 G2 Nitrolon high output flashlight with extra batteries: *Only use in signaling help; again, reverse the batteries*
- TV/weather/AM/FM radio Walkman with extra batteries: *I chose Sony SRF-M37V*
- 3 candles
- Cotton balls soaked in Vaseline: *Great for starting fires; keep them in leftover film containers (I learned this one from Laurence Gonzales)*
- 2 Bic lighters
- Waterproof matches
- Windproof/waterproof butane lighter and extra butane
- Magnesium fire-starting tool
- Magnifying glass
- Whistle
- Mace or pepper spray: *Personal protection against man and animal (Personal protection is an individual issue, and the laws vary from state to state, and country to country. Here you are on your own.)*
- 3 carabiners: *Don't skimp; you may need them for more than hanging a water bottle from your pack*
- Small (non-aerosol) bug repellent with Deet

- Small stick of sunscreen, 36+: *I like Bullfrog brand*
- Compass: *Don't skimp on the quality, and keep the directions*
- Emergency reflector blanket 53" x 82" or bigger
- Waterproof tarp (Wxtex makes a great one) or plastic drop cloth, heavy duty, 2 mil, 9' x 12': *These should fold up tightly for packing*
- 2 lengths of nylon parachute cord, ¼" x 10' and ¼" x 12
- 2 fluorescent light sticks
- Soap (antibacterial)
- Small binoculars
- Leatherman Tool: *I like the Wave model*
- Knife and sharpener: *If folding, must have locked position*
- Titanium or enamel cup: *Make sure you can cook with it*
- Spork (spoon/fork combination)
- Safety pins, medium size
- Dental floss: *Unflavored waxed floss is good for heavy-duty sewing*
- 1 pair of leather work gloves
- Duct tape
- Nose and mouth protection: *I use a formed cotton painter's mask, but a good one*
- Prepaid phone card and change: *Cell phones run out of battery power, but there's always a chance that regular phone lines will work*

Fishing Equipment *(Think about the environment you'll be in, freshwater versus saltwater)*

- Fishing line, 20 lb test 110 yd spool
- Hooks
- Lead weights

- Bobbers
- Flies: *I carry a small assortment of both saltwater and freshwater flies; this item is not entirely necessary*
- 2 pocket fly fishing guides, 1 for freshwater and 1 for saltwater: *Again, this item is not entirely necessary*

Medical Supplies *(Lofty says, "What you include depends upon your own skill using it")*

- Antibiotic: *I chose Ciprofloxin 500 mg x 30*
- Analgesic: *I chose Advil and Hydrocodone*
- Antihistamine: *I chose Benadryl*
- Antidiarrheal: *I chose Imodium A-D*
- Antibiotic ointment: *I chose Neosporin*
- Band-Aids Tough-Strips Waterproof
- Butterfly sutures: *You can also make these from Band-Aids*
- Tweezers
- Epi pen
- Needles and button/carpet weight thread
- Self-adhering Ace bandage
- 1 roll sports tape
- Multivitamins
- Any medications that are life sustaining to you as an individual

Food *(Calorie-dense foods that are high in fat; the only problem is these don't have a long shelf life)*

- Electrolyte powder: *I chose Trace Mineral Stamina Electrolyte*
- Beef jerky, vacuum packed
- Calorie-dense nutritional bars
- Nut and dried fruit mix
- Tea bags: *Earl Grey—my luxury item!*

There are a million and one different items you could include, depending on the circumstances or environment you might encounter. But these are the top essentials for both urban and wilderness survival. Be sure to keep the directions for any item you're not completely familiar with, but—even better—spend some time learning to use each item. Try to start a fire with the magnesium firestarter, and try to filter water with your MiniWorks water filter. This will build your knowledge base and increase your chances of survival if you ever do need the pack.

Store your pack in a relatively cool environment (not in the trunk of your car in hundred-degree weather), and keep it handy but away from animals and small children. Remember that some items have expiration dates and will need to be replaced on occasion.

Knowledge is a key ingredient in survival, so read up on the topic. Over the years, I've collected a variety of books on survival. Besides Lofty's book, two others I think are a must are *Deep Survival* by Laurence Gonzales (and not just because I'm in it; it's a fascinating book that will teach you how the mind works when in survival mode and basically explains who lives and who dies) and *Camping and Wilderness Survival* by Paul Tawrell.

Bruce Nussbaum in his article "The Next Big One" (*BusinessWeek*, September 19, 2005) explains that "The good news is that preparing for one disaster prepares for all of them." I truly hope that none of us ever needs this survival kit. But in this world, you just never know. What I do know is this: being prepared physically is all part of being prepared mentally. If you're ready, this will significantly increase your chances for survival.